Future Choice

Why Network Marketing May Be Your *Best* Career Move

Michael S. Clouse
Kathie Jackson Anderson

**Introduction by
Scott DeGarmo, Editor-in-Chief
& Publisher, *SUCCESS* magazine**

Future Choice
Why Network Marketing May Be Your *BEST* Career Move
Michael S. Clouse
Kathie Jackson Anderson

Upline® Press

Third Edition Copyright ©1996
by Michael S. Clouse and Kathie Jackson Anderson
All rights reserved.
Published by *Upline®* Press
400 East Jefferson Street, Charlottesville, VA 22902
(804) 979-4427   FAX (804) 979-1602
http://www.uplineonline.com

Manufactured in the United States of America

ISBN: 0-9634259-9-4
Library of Congress Catalog Card Number: 93-070272

Table of Contents

Introduction

I HEARTILY RECOMMEND THIS APTLY TITLED and well-written book to anyone seeking to learn about opportunities in Network Marketing.

I personally learned about the power of Network Marketing somewhat reluctantly. Like so many people, my mind was mainly closed on the subject. Then one of my editors at *SUCCESS* began urging me to let him do a report for our readers on the topic. I explained to the staffer that, based on what little I knew, I had a hard time believing that Network Marketing could be seen as a serious way of building a business or making a living. "Some of the stories are simply too good to be true," I said, attempting to close the matter.

As it happened, I was dealing with Senior Editor Richard Poe, who had spent months examining the issue and preparing arguments to present to me and my other editors. In our ensuing editorial meetings, as Poe recounted statistics, case studies and anecdotes, I found myself becoming more receptive to his proposal.

However, some staffers considered the entire subject one to be shunned. As the opposing editors sensed my interest in the topic growing, they called a "time out" so they could gather material to present the opposite point of view. With the help of our researchers and our Nexus on-line service, our offices were soon flooded with Network Marketing articles from the national press. I read stacks of them, noting how public officials and regulators frequently made critical comments about Network Marketing or multi-level marketing, as it is often called.

But what all the previous coverage demonstrated to me was different from what my staff critics had intended. What the articles made clear was that the other side of the story—the positive side—had never been told. Why was this the case? Because the press in general, and the business press in particular, is, by and large, not opportunity-oriented. The journalistic mindset is inclined to be skeptical, critical, doubting, analytical—all important traits, to be sure. But what was needed to see the Network Marketing story was a receptive, entrepreneurial, future-oriented perspective—a mindset that seeks out what is good in an idea. Moreover, I concluded, the positive story was going to be a far more important one in the long run.

The article that was eventually published in *SUCCESS* was the first fundamentally positive treatment of Network Marketing to appear in a major national publication. We pointed out how Network Marketing has often been wrongly confused with illegal pyramid schemes that convince people they can make money without working. We interviewed a range of experts, including Dr. Srikimar Rao, chairman of the marketing department at Long Island University and a student of MLM companies for nearly two decades. Dr. Rao began studying the field because he was aware that it had been ignored by mainstream researchers. Rao was one of the first academics to realize the enormous power of Network Marketing to create wealth. Our article also demonstrated how Network Marketing was being fueled by a pervasive sense of insecurity, an observation that seems more timely than ever today as we continue to witness tens of thousands of workers losing their jobs. Happily, many of these workers will find financial reward and personal freedom in Network Marketing.

Our conclusion was that Network Marketing is a powerful method of doing business that would grow in importance in the coming decade. The response to our coverage was so overwhelming that we have since made Network Marketing an ongoing part of our editorial coverage. Up to now, no book for the general public has appeared on the subject. So, the publication of *Future Choice* is a significant event.

Scott DeGarmo

Scott DeGarmo
Editor-in-Chief & Publisher
SUCCESS magazine

Preface

IN HIS BOOK, *All I Really Need to Know I Learned in Kindergarten*, author-philosopher Robert Fulghum tells the story of when Halley's Comet swept across our skies in 1910:

"The world was divided between those who celebrated and those who watched in fear and trembling," Fulghum wrote. Those who knew and understood the comet watched its fiery approach with awe and anticipation. Those who didn't watched in fear and dread. They all experienced the same comet, but in completely different ways.

You always have the opportunity to live your life in those same two ways; in knowledgeable anticipation or in ignorance and fear.

It is a choice which shapes your future.

It is your *Future Choice*.

Our goal in *Future Choice* is to introduce you to one unique opportunity for your life and work—Network Marketing. As you consider whether Network Marketing may the best career move for you, we hope we can in some small way help you to be one of those men and women who choose their futures with knowledgeable anticipation.

1
2003, A Story

"By 1960, work will be limited
to three hours a day."
— John Langdon-Davies,
A Short History of the Future, 1936

Susan Edison leaned against the doorway as she looked across the deck of her Colorado home to the wildflower-filled meadows and majestic mountains beyond.

She sighed with contentment, then turned back into the house reaching for her coffee cup as she moved through the bright, sunny kitchen into the living room.

Speaking commands to her video home theater, Susan instantly called up a hologram network and selected a style of sofa she'd been thinking of buying. Immediately, the form of the couch appeared in the room, in just the fabric she had requested.

Susan studied the three-dimensional sofa for a minute, then shook her head a little moving the theater's control to position the seemingly solid hologram closer to the fireplace. A double-click on the remote changed the sofa's fabric to one that more closely reflected the shades of the spring flowers outside

Susan smiled. Yes, that was just right.

She moved the remote back to the video screen, clicked once, ordering the sofa and clicked again to request express home delivery. Satisfied, she spoke a command to turn off the video display.

Although the sofa disappeared, Susan knew it would be there in her living room home in just two days.

Susan smiled again, thinking of Jennifer Wellington, her dentist, who would receive a commission on the purchase of the sofa.

In addition to her dental practice, Jennifer represented a company that offered a complete line of home furnishings. By buying her sofa through Jennifer's satellite hologram network, Susan saved the extra cost of buying her furniture through one of the few retail stores that remained. Shopping this way also allowed her to support Jennifer, who in return was one of her own best customers.

Susan cast one last glance around her living room, pleased with the decision she had made that morning, then she walked across the hallway to her office. Only 10 minutes remained until her first conference of the day.

That morning Susan spoke with six of her top business associates in a nationwide video conference call. She addressed 1,500 new prospects through a two-way video link broadcast each Tuesday morning over her own personal channel on her company's direct satellite network. And with a single push of a button, she sent her weekly newsletter by electronic mail to 30,000 of her own distributors throughout the world.

After lunch on her deck, Susan strolled down into the meadow. The children would be home soon. This was her best chance for a few minutes to herself after a busy morning.

She'd come a long way in the last nine years, since 1994 when she first began her own home-based business. And all because she'd listened to a friend who had told her about a new way of doing business.

Again, Susan smiled.

I T MAY BE THE NEW AMERICAN DREAM. 1990s style. No boss, set your own hours, succeed or fail by your own efforts. All with a computer, a cordless phone and a fax machine. Preferably from the sunny deck of your new custom built home.

According to *USA Today*, as many as 96 percent of adults ages 25–44 are "very interested" in owning their own business. Today, more than 42.3 million people work at home, full- or part-time, as self-employed business entrepreneurs or telecommuters. Millions of people design boats, make wine, create manuscripts or broker information from a re-designed corner in the garage or a spare room in the house.

Hewlett-Packard, Apple Computers, Mrs. Fields' Cookies, Domino's Pizza, Nike and Walt Disney Productions all started as home-based businesses, say Paul and Sarah Edwards, themselves home-based authors of a series of best-selling books on self-employment. Whether your dream is to catapult your own company into the Fortune 500 or to blend home life and work life into one seamless existence, business forecasters say today's updated version of home-based entrepreneurship may be the best model for the businesses of the future.

"There are two ways to the CEO's chair," write Patricia Aburdene and John Naisbitt in their book, *Megatrends for Women.* "The corporate route: Draw up a five- or ten-year plan to gather the skills for the top-executive job you hope to land in, say, 1998 or 2003. And the entrepreneurial approach: Start

3

your own business now."

At the turn of this century, as many as 50 percent of U.S. adults were self-employed. And the Edwardses predict, by the turn of the next century, they may be again.

Self-employment hit its low point in the 1970s, at 7 million. But by 1980, that number had climbed to 8.6 million and by 1994, the number of self-employed in the U.S. had increased to 10.65 million people. And the numbers continue to rise.

Several business trends are converging to spur a return to self-employment. One is the economy itself.

As we continue the conversion from an industrial society to one based on information and services, the way North Americans earn their living is changing as well. Yet for too many of us, the change has been pretty painful.

Fortune 500 companies shed 9 million jobs during the past decade. Corporations such as General Motors, IBM and AT&T, once considered a ticket to lifelong employment security, are jettisoning middle-management layers and the employees that go with them by the tens of thousands.

In an effort to find a place in the evolving global economy, companies are selling off or closing down plants or entire divisions. They are centralizing and economizing, outsourcing and contracting. Entire industries are disappearing and taking with them the security of those who depended on them for their life's work.

As corporations continue to consolidate operations, labor analysts say the number of corporate-based jobs will continue to decline. "The bond of loyalty between employer and employee has been broken by the merger mania and the 'lean and mean' response to global competition," writes Gerald Celente, a New York-based trends analyst in his book, *Trend Tracking*.

"If you work for a corporation, you can no longer sit back and enjoy the comfort of job security. If you're a top executive, you may have a golden parachute that will give you a nice soft landing. But if you're a senior executive, a middle manager or just an employee, you have nothing to protect you other than your ability to get a job somewhere else."

But where else?

And at what salary?

Many of yesterday's higher-paying manufacturing jobs now live overseas and still others are packing their bags for the trip abroad.

Since 1965, U.S. corporations have built more that 1,800 plants—employing more than 500,000 workers—in neighboring Mexico alone. That figure is expected to climb to almost 4,500 plants by 1997, according to projections by the Secretariat of Commerce and Industrial Development in Mexico City. While their public relations officers say they regret the impact on U.S. workers, companies as diverse as Zenith and Fisher-Price say if they want to remain competitive they have no choice but to move to countries where wage rates are lower.

For the first time in our economic history, the cutbacks are slicing as deep into executive suites as they have into blue-collar production lines. Bank presidents, stock analysts and entire corporate public relations departments are now just as likely as a GM auto worker to find themselves suddenly unemployed.

Whatever the job classification, the contraction is not confined to marginal employees with limited skills. Today's unemployment lines are full of bright, motivated and engaging people—people who have much to offer. Unfortunately, the loss of their jobs is not temporary, nor is it part of a typical, short-term business cycle. Most of the jobs lost in the last decade will not return.

NORTH AMERICANS HAVE COME TO RELY on a three-legged financial stool to provide them with financial security: A private pension, Social Security and their personal savings. But for both men and women, that formula has all but disappeared.

Personal debt remains at an all-time high and the U.S. national savings rate remains among the lowest in the industrialized world. Even workers who expect to receive a full pension at retirement are not assured a comfortable life. Labor Department statistics show that in 1994 the median private pension for married men was $4,562 a year, or less that $88 a week; for married women it was $2,389 a year, or $45.94 a week.

More than whether average pension rates are too low, the question is whether those who have counted on a pension will actually receive one at all?

According to the Federal Reserve and the Bureau of Labor Statistics, corporate debt climbed from $10,000 per employee in 1950, to $23,387 per employee by the end of the 1980s. Some ompanies took on the debt to finance a fight against corporate raiders; others were loaded with debt and stripped of assets after they fell victim. Either way, in a desperate search for cash to pay the interest on their debt, too many corporations went looking in the one place that was earlier sacrosanct—their once protected pension funds.

"Corporations removed $21 billion from their employees' pension plans during the 1980s; overall, nearly 2,000 corporations dipped into employee pension funds for at least $1 million each," write Philadelphia Inquirer investigative reporters Donald Barlett and James Steele in their Pulitzer Prize-winning book, *America: What Went Wrong?*

When government moved to protect private pensions with laws that regulated pension-raiding, many companies made an end run around the new regulations by abandoning traditional corporate pensions altogether.

It seems the traditional three-legged stool of financial security has developed a marked wobble—if not fallen down altogether.

THAT FINANCIAL WOBBLE IS ONE REASON millions of North Americans are choosing to embrace a newly designed economic stool—one with four solid legs on the ground.

That fourth leg, is ownership of their own full- or part-time home-based business.

And today record numbers of us *are* choosing to chart our own economic future, to live by our own business wits.

By the end of 1995, 44 percent of all U.S. households had an income-producing or after-hours home office, generating revenue of approximately $382.5 billion annually. And those numbers continue to climb.

Some of today's new business owners want to build an empire, like Walt Disney, Colonel Sanders or Steven Jobs. Others want only to make a second income, one that will provide the difference between living and truly living well.

Financial experts say the quality of life for millions of North Americans would increase significantly if they were just able to increase their monthly income by $200 to $500 a month. That's enough to start an investment account or to buy a more reliable car. And it's more than enough to begin piano lessons, take the family to Disney World or pay off a credit card.

All this and more, is possible. Because between today's economic uncertainty and our futuristic friend—21st century entrepreneur Susan Edison—lies one of the business world's best kept secrets. And certainly one of its most profound and potent opportunities.

2
A Business of Your Own

"Money can do good, great good . . . Properly
placed financial incentives can get the best out
of people. The power of money steers medical
research and fuels the arts."
— Edward D. Hallowell, M.D. and William
J. Grace, Jr., in *What Are You Worth?*

I N 1986, EUNICE VINBERG baby-sat part-time in her home
to make a little extra money. Today, she earns more than
the president of the United States. Much more. Her income just bought her family a sprawling new home in the
suburbs of Seattle, and her husband, a youth pastor, now
works because he loves his job—not because he needs to.

The Vinbergs used spunk and energy to turn a hot idea
into a career, the classic talent of a successful entrepreneur.

Eunice and Emil Vinberg are the top U.S. sales representatives for a California-based company that distributes high-end
Japanese skincare and cosmetics. Noevir, one of the largest di-
rect-marketed companies in Japan, uses personal representatives
to sell its products. The Vinbergs now work through an international system of distributors that they, or those independent

contractors in their Network, introduced to their company.

The Vinbergs are paid a commission on all their retail sales and a bonus on all purchases made within their Network organization. They make more money in a month than most people make in a year by introducing people to their company and by teaching and motivating them to duplicate their own success.

"Before I became involved, I basically thought this business was for people who couldn't get a real job," says Susan Davidson of West Vancouver, British Columbia, who not long ago started her own home-based business. "Then, I trusted a friend, got involved and one year later—as a single mom with three kids— I had earned more than $200,000."

Growing numbers of people like Susan Davidson and the Vinbergs are looking at the other side of today's global economic uncertainty—the opportunity side. Their home-based businesses allow them to understand and take advantage of today's business trends—not to fear them. They're building long-term residual income and personal freedom using a business concept known today as Network Marketing.

NETWORK MARKETING, sometimes called multi-level marketing or MLM, is one of several ways to move products from manufacturers to consumers. Although Network Marketing is not a new concept, it is not yet well understood.

Network Marketing is an alternative distribution system to those used by most major corporations in North America today. While other more common forms of distribution are under stress—witness the rash of bankruptcies in the wholesale/retail industry—Network Marketing is expanding rapidly.

To illustrate why, let's take a look at some of the methods companies have developed to move their products from the manufacturer to the consumer. The most well known of course, is the retail channel.

Corporations spend enormous amounts of money, sometimes as much as $10 or $20 million per advertising campaign, to make you want to buy what they have to sell. Advertising may make you laugh or may make you grit your teeth, but if it gets you to leave your house in search of what the company is selling, it's a success.

Yet the cost of all that advertising is only the beginning. Long before you've even warmed up your car, or before your children have badgered you into promising them the latest TV-inspired fad, those companies have sold their products—at a profit, of course—to wholesalers and distributors across the country.

Wholesalers pay another entire layer of middlemen—truckers and warehouse workers and clerical employees, etc. And then add their costs and their profits to the price of the item you want to buy.

Your increasingly more expensive product next moves into the retail store where, in many industries, wholesalers must pay an additional heavy "slotting" fee to win the product a space on a retail shelf. That fee, like all the others, gets passed on to you. So does the cost of the store's advertising, its light bill and the cost of its employees' health insurance, vacations and "shrinkage"—another word for what gets broken or stolen.

It shouldn't surprise you then if you—the shopper that all these people spent millions of dollars to attract—hear an almost audible sigh of relief across the retail landscape when you pull into a mall parking lot.

Yet you may not.

You may be too busy searching for a parking place or negotiating through a maze of store corridors specifically designed to confuse you. If you do reach your item of interest, you will then wait in line to pay for it, balancing your purchase in one hand while you attempt to reach for your two forms of identification with the other.

There must be a better way, and consumers are constantly searching for it.

Each week, millions of North Americans travel to large discount warehouse stores where buying clubs offer rock bottom prices on mass merchandise to qualified members in exchange for a small annual fee. These shoppers choose to trade service and convenience for value.

Others find they prefer shopping by catalog. A handful of large general department stores have operated giant catalog divisions for years. Their catalogs offer thousands of items for sale direct from the company's warehouses. If they have your size, if the style you want isn't backordered and if you don't mind returning to the store four days later to pick it up, you're in great shape.

Some specialty companies, such as L.L. Bean, have refined the art of shopping by catalog even further and market it as a more pleasant alternative to retail shopping.

Often known for the excellent service they provide, a number of such mail-order companies have developed followings of loyal customers who look forward to receiving each catalog. Their products often are of a quality and selection unavailable in most retail stores, and their goods often are shipped to buyers' homes, with 100 percent satisfaction guaranteed.

Network Marketing seeks to combine the best aspects of all these distribution systems—the high quality merchandise offered by the best specialty stores, the convenience of catalog shopping, the cost savings of direct selling, and the ease and time-saving value of to-your-door delivery. Then it takes the concept one step further. Network Marketing pays you to participate in its form of sales and distribution.

SUCESS MAGAZINE CALLS NETWORK MARKETING "the most powerful way to reach consumers in the '90s." Dozens of the nation's most innovative companies are taking a closer look at Network Marketing, because it is the one delivery method of goods and services that complements the world's developing business trends.

"Manufacturers are looking for a way to spend advertising dollars as close to the point of sale as possible," writes business author Charles Whitlock in his book, *How To Get Rich*.

"That's what Network Marketing does: it provides a one-on-one sales presentation to potential customers right at the point of sale. A person who wants to buy doesn't have to turn off the TV and go to the market, dial an 800 number or mail anything in. All the customer has to do is say, "Yes." And the customer is likely to say, "Yes," because MLM distributors are usually among the most enthusiastic and committed sales professionals in the marketplace."

Today a consumer can buy almost anything through Network Marketing, from life insurance to satellite television to health food. And a number of the nation's most successful corporations have built their business solely by Network Marketing. Other Fortune 500 companies have complete Network Marketing subsidiaries, including Colgate-Palmolive and Gillette. Rexall Drugs, one of the country's best-known retail names, has created a new division, Rexall Showcase International, to offer health and wellness products through Network

13

Marketing. Other companies are creating partnerships with Network Marketing companies as well . . .

MCI turned to Amway Corp. and Sprint to Network 2000, to market their long distance services through those companies' nationwide networks of independent distributors. These joint ventures worked. Three million (3,000,000) subscribers later, AT&T, stung by the potency of Network Marketing, launched its "We want you back" advertising campaign.

SOME OF THE HIGHEST QUALITY and most innovative products over the years have been marketed solely through independent Network distributors. Can openers, chewing gum, microwave ovens, razors, sewing machines, smoke detectors and vacuum cleaners all were first introduced into the marketplace through direct selling channels.

Business analysts predict the amount of goods and services that move through Network channels will increase at a rate of as much as 30 percent per year in the next few years, many times the rate of growth predicted for the economy as a whole. Part of the reason is that the products most commonly marketed today through Network Marketing channels are those that will be appealing to the baby boom generation as they move through middle age.

Trend trackers say baby boomers are searching for fitness, vitality, youthful appearances and convenience. They crave products that will make them healthy and attractive. They want quality products *and* perceived value. Yet they're willing to pay for what they want, even in lean times, because they feel they deserve it.

Internationally known futurist Faith Popcorn calls this trend "egonomics."

"It's about individuating, differentiating, customizing," she writes in her bestseller, *The Popcorn Report.* "And it's a major force to reckon with in today's marketplace. Egonomics means simply this: there is profit to be reaped in providing for the consumer's need for personalization, whether it be in product concept, product design, or personal service."

Network Marketing companies have been on the forefront of those trends for years with all-natural food supplements, organically grown packaged food, herbal cosmetic and skincare lines and earth friendly recyclable packaging. As this massive group of consumers moves into the most vibrant and active middle years yet known, Networking companies await them with products to help retain their zest, lose excess weight, fight wrinkles and insure the quality of their lives.

According to Popcorn's research, in the decade of the 1990s, people are also "retrenching."

They see the frenzy in their lives and they are looking for ways to create a more serene and prosperous future for themselves and those they love. They are searching for ways to build that future without sacrificing themselves and their values in the process.

It's a movement authors Patricia Aburdene and John Naisbitt call the search for opportunity, leadership and balance. It is a search for ways to work smarter, live smarter and make smarter choices, so there is more left to give to families, to the world and to one another. It is a desire to create something of value and integrity with which to shape a future of joy and prosperity.

For millions of people, that's just the opportunity Network Marketing offers.

3

One Plus One

"Leisure time, not money, is becoming
the status symbol of the 1990s."
— John P. Robinson, University of Maryland researcher

IN 1991, DARRYL AND LYNN KUNTZ of Rockwall, Texas,
were living the new American dream.
They had made the leap small business advocates Paul and
Sarah Edwards had predicted, to a home-based business of their
own. As successful movie producers, the Kuntzes specialized in
family movies and videos for national distribution. Lynn Kuntz
wrote the script for their largest production, *"Dakota,"* a movie
that opened nationwide in 1988 starring Lou Diamond Phillips.

They worked from twin offices in their lakeside country
home. Their business allowed them to work together and to be
deeply involved with their four children, yet by the early 1990s,
Darryl and Lynn had decided they needed to rethink the direc-
tion of their business. Each movie project meant raising millions of dollars from investors and in an economically darkened
nation, investment capital was becoming harder to find.

"We were looking to diversify," Lynn Kuntz says. "We were
especially interested in residual income. We sat down and tried

to think what qualities we would look for in a second business. "We had been in business for a number of years," she says. "We knew the amount of paperwork involved, the time devoted to keeping track of taxes and accounting. We were looking for something that would not include the 'busyness' of a small business. We wanted something that would allow us to work together—Darryl and I have always worked together—and we wanted something with the potential for serious growth. If you're going to invest your time and effort, you want the opportunity to find the gold at the end of the rainbow. We were looking for something that was seemingly impossible."

Perhaps not.

A wealthy business associate who had been an investor in their film projects introduced them to Network Marketing. "We called him and asked if we could attend one of his meetings," Lynn says. "We made it clear we were not interested in joining his company. We were considering whether we would be able to develop a Network Marketing program to distribute our films.

"We went, and we were so impressed when we realized what the business trends were and what the income potential was."

That night, the Kuntzes realized that Network Marketing met all their criteria for an additional business venture. Not long after the meeting, the Kuntzes discovered a company that distributes high technology skincare products developed by a world-renowned scientist. After thoroughly investigating the company, its products and leadership, the Kuntzes joined. Today their "downline," those to whom they have introduced the concept, is one of their company's largest groups.

As experienced business people, the Kuntzes took a clear, close look at Network Marketing before deciding it was the opportunity they sought. "We were not looking for this at all,"

Lynn says. "We've been surprised at how much we enjoy Network Marketing. We consider ourselves creative people, and there are so many creative ways to build our business. We don't feel we have put our creativity aside at all."

The Kuntzes have been approached about other film projects, but for now they have decided to focus on building their Networking business.

"We feel like the ball is really rolling with this now," Lynn Kuntz says. "We believe we'll be able to build an income that will allow us to finance our own films sometime in the future. But it's not like we're working at this until we're able to do what we really want. We love this. Someday later on we may decide to do a film project. We'll do both."

THE KUNTZES ARE NOT ALONE in their move into Network Marketing. The Direct Selling Association, one of several industry associations, estimates $17.94 billion of goods and services were sold in the U.S. by Network Marketing Direct Selling companies in 1995, while the World-Wide Federation of Direct Selling Associations (WFDSA) reported international sales of $72.18 billion. That amount has grown by more than $9 billion since 1987 in the U.S. alone.

In 1995, 25 million people in more that 125 countries were estimated to have earned an income from Network Marketing Direct Sales, and those numbers continue to grow at the rate of 150,000 new people per week!

"I use to think the only way to enjoy the lifestyle I really wanted was to work two or three jobs at the same time. But, now I know the truth," says Kay Smith, owner of her own Networking business. "My seven-figure annual income and the free time to enjoy it are living proof that in Network Marketing, you really can have it all."

The first experience many have with Network Marketing is when they are approached by someone they know with an opportunity to buy products from the company that person represents. Millions of people have purchased products or services from a Network entrepreneur. Even if they make purchases at first primarily to show support for a friend's new business venture, they often later find themselves returning when they discover the value and quality of those products and services.

There are three common ways to participate in Network Marketing:

1. As a wholesale buyer. Many of those involved in Network Marketing sign up with a company for the benefit of buying its products wholesale. Wholesale consumers purchase products primarily for themselves and their families. Typically, they pay a nominal annual fee, much like the membership fees charged by wholesale buying clubs, to buy their products at a reduced cost directly from the company itself or from their "sponsor," the person who introduced them to the company and its products.

2. As a part-time Networker. Like wholesale buyers, part-time Networkers buy and use their company's products for themselves and their families. In addition, they also tell some of their friends, neighbors or relatives about their savings on a casual basis. They introduce a few others to the company and help them sign up to receive the same product discounts they enjoy. They then receive a bonus, typically a small percentage of the total sales of everyone they sponsor into the company's marketing program.

Many professional Networkers who go on to earn large

monthly bonuses, like the Vinbergs, who we met earlier, typically begin as wholesale buyers or as part-time Networkers. In a recent survey, the Direct Selling Association estimated that almost 90 percent of all Networkers work their business only part-time.

Experienced Networkers tell us, part-time Networkers can expect to build incomes of from $200 to $500 a month or more as their Networks grow. Those who build sizeable Network organizations or who sponsor others who do so, can earn incomes many times that.

Thousands of part-time Networking professionals are matching—sometimes a number of times over—the salaries they earn at their full-time jobs. People begin in a Network Marketing business with the idea of making $100, $300 or even $500 per month. Suddenly they realize that if they become serious about their business, they could make $1,000 or $2,000 per month or more.

3. *As a full-time Networker.* Those who decide to build a full-time Network Marketing business buy and use their company's products for themselves and their families. In addition, they work full-time to tell others about their company, its products and the business opportunity it presents.

"When I first signed up with Mary Kay, reactions ranged from doubtful to very, very doubtful," recounts Shirley Hutton in her book, *Pay Yourself What You're Worth.* Hutton moved from a career in television as host of a TV talk show to representing industry giant Mary Kay Cosmetics.

"My husband thought I'd lost my mind. My daughter Elizabeth was shocked and the other three children more or less snickered," she says. Within the first three months, Shirley Hutton saw more gaped jaws than any dentist.

But not for long. In the first few years of Hutton's new venture, her income rose to more than $400,000 a year.

Network Marketing's advantage is its ability to compensate company representatives not only for their own efforts, but also for the efforts of those they bring into their Network organization, even into fourth, fifth and subsequent levels of participation. Network Marketing companies use the money more traditional companies spend on advertising and distribution to pay commissions and bonuses to their representatives, to those who are promoting their products directly to the market place.

It's called the exponential success path. And it is open to any Network Marketer—wholesale, part-time or full-time—sometimes with astounding results. Today, Network Marketers across the country, and around the world are earning $10,000, $30,000, $75,000 and more. Per month.

NETWORKERS USE TWO FAVORITE EXAMPLES to explain Networking's exponential compensation system. The first is called the doubling concept. Here's an example:

Take one penny and set it aside. The next day, and every day thereafter, double the number of pennies you set aside.

It's simple. On the second day, you will have two cents; on the third day, four cents. By the end of the first week, you will have 64 cents. Now fasten your financial seat belt.

By the end of the second week, you will have accumulated $81.92. By the end of the third week, more than $10,000 and by the end of the month, you will have saved well over $5 million and will be scrambling for storage space for all those pennies.

Turn the pennies into people generating bonuses on product sales and turn the days into weeks or months, and the economic power of Network Marketing begins to emerge.

Here's how doubling might work in real life, using Network Marketing's second common example:

Suppose that after learning about the power of Network Marketing and finding a company whose products you believe in, you pay a nominal fee—usually under $100—to become a distributor.

In the first month, you tell your friends and family about your new venture and about the exciting benefits of the products you represent. You are able to save money buying the products you use at wholesale prices, and you make an immediate profit by selling some products at retail prices to those who want to buy directly from you.

Now suppose that, in addition, you find one person who would like to join you, someone who also recognizes the potential of Network Marketing and who wants to do what you are doing.

At the end of your first month, in addition to saving money by purchasing your products wholesale and making profits from your own retail sales, you would also be earning bonuses on all the sales of the person you sponsored into the organization.

That's the beginning of what Network Marketers call a "downline." You have two people in your organization—yourself and your first sponsored colleague. One plus one makes two. Maybe. *(see Figure 1)*

To continue the example, what if in the second month you sponsor one other person into your organization? And the person you sponsored sponsors one person. Suddenly you have four people in your organization and you're earning bonuses on the

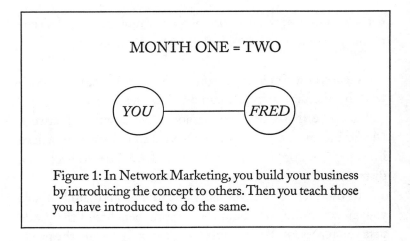

MONTH ONE = TWO

Figure 1: In Network Marketing, you build your business by introducing the concept to others. Then you teach those you have introduced to do the same.

sales of all those people, yet you yourself sponsored only two people *(see Figure 2)*.

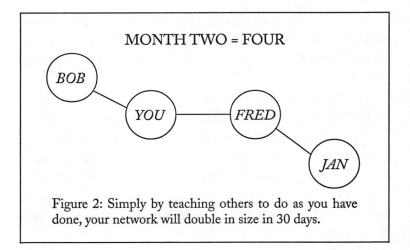

MONTH TWO = FOUR

Figure 2: Simply by teaching others to do as you have done, your network will double in size in 30 days.

Again, in the third month of your business, you sponsor one person. So do each of those already in your group. Now you've grown to eight: you, the three people you have sponsored directly and the four others they have introduced to your business. Remember, this all could be happening before most other start-up businesses have earned a single penny of profit *(see Figure 3)*.

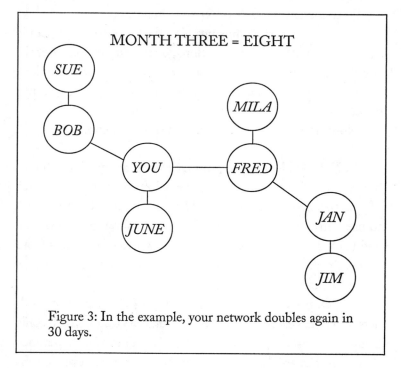

MONTH THREE = EIGHT

Figure 3: In the example, your network doubles again in 30 days.

To show the true power of Network Marketing, let's follow the example a little further.

Suppose you, as a part-time or full-time Network entrepreneur, decide to find more than one person a month to join you in your business. Suppose instead of just one person, you sponsor two people each month who want to build a business as you are doing.

25

You sponsor two people the first month, who sponsor two the next, who teach their two to sponsor two. By the end of four months, you have 30 active people in your group, yet you yourself have sponsored only one more person each month.

Take the examples two steps further.

If you, as a serious business-builder, sponsor four people each month with similar ambitions, by the end of four months you will enjoy a Network of 256 committed business builders. If you sponsor five, that number explodes to 625. Yet you personally sponsor only five people each month.

Now, here's where your efforts turn into income.

In Network Marketing, you receive compensation, called a bonus, from the sale of all products within your group. If each of your 625 people buys only $100 worth of products per month to use personally, to share as gifts and to show to others, you and your group will have sold $62,500 worth of products. Your bonus check could easily reach above $7,000, depending on the compensation plan of your company.

If each person in your group buys only $50 worth of products or services each month, that still totals $31,250, which could bring you substantially more than $3,000 a month. Remember, that's without any "sales superstars," any extra-achievers or any large amount of retail sales. That's you and five of your colleagues teaching those you sponsor to build their organizations just as you have yours each purchasing only $50 every month. (see *Figure 4*)

Figure 4. Look what would happen if you introduced five people into your business and taught each one to do the same. At the end of four months, you would have almost 800 people in your network.

		Total number in your group
You ...		
teach five ...	(5)	6
how to teach five ...	(25)	31
to each sponsor five ...	(125)	156
who will each sponsor five.	(625)	781

Network Marketers across the country are using concepts just like these to build substantial incomes for themselves and their families. As we continue, let's look more closely at how.

4
Profits and Prosperity

"In the 90s, instead of going to the
store, the store will come to us."
— Faith Popcorn, *The Popcorn Report*

NOT YET 30 YEARS OLD, Jason Boreyko is a Network Marketing phenomenon. He built his Networking success story at an age when many young people are still trying to decide what to do with their lives.

Boreyko was making $2 an hour as a valet in a large hotel when he began his Network Marketing career. His boss, he says, practically pushed him into it.

"I asked for a 25-cent an hour raise," Boreyko says. "After two years I wanted to go from $2 to $2.25. " His boss turned him down.

"That's when I said, 'Hey I've got to do something else.'"

Boreyko knew about Network Marketing: his parents had been involved in the business. With a goal in mind, to prove his boss wrong, Boreyko set out to build his own business.

"Sure, I had ups and downs," he says. "After about five months, I almost quit the industry. But I had nothing to go back to."

Once Boreyko found the company that clicked for him, there was no looking back. "I started with a $2,000-a-month goal," he says. "It took me eight months to reach that goal." In two years, Boreyko was making $10,000 a month.

"The first year I struggled," he says. "The second year, I broke six figures."

Boreyko had built his business to $30,000 a month by the time he bumped into his old boss. His former employer soon joined him in his business.

"Age really isn't a barrier," Boreyko says of his early start in Network Marketing. "The desire to change your life has to be there. I'm just an average guy. I didn't go to college; I didn't have the opportunity.

"To be honest, at first I did it for the money. But today, my greatest satisfaction is helping other people achieve their financial dreams. Like my father says, if you want to be a chief, you have to be a servant to many."

Boreyko has found a level of business success most in the corporate world only dream of. His largest monthly check, so far, has been $63,000.

How is that possible?

Leading Networkers across the country are making $10,000, $30,000, $75,000 per month, by putting two concepts, exponential growth and indirect compensation, to work in their businesses.

As we described earlier, all Network Marketing companies compensate their representatives through some form of exponential bonus payment. As a distributor, you receive commissions on your sales and bonuses on all purchases made in your group. Your income grows as the amount of product sold by members of your group grows. Your compensation is directly linked to your efforts, not to some artificial outside evaluation of how much your skills and talents are worth, as is often the case with a traditional salary.

There is no limit to how well your efforts can be rewarded. There are no salary freezes or caps, no waiting to see if your company will offer a production bonus. Office politics play no part in your compensation; neither does favoritism.

With indirect compensation, you once again profit not only from your own work, but from the work of a growing number of others, as well. You're on the same team, and joint team goals build strong partnerships. *You* benefit from the work of your associates; you all benefit from the effort *you* contribute.

As you learn your business, you teach, coach and motivate the other members of your team. They become more effective businesses owners in their own right and all of you experience greater prosperity and higher levels of accomplishment. As their businesses grow, they do the same with their teams. They continue your legacy of success and you all continue to prosper.

Once you establish your Network, you can go on vacation, care for a sick child, visit family, go on a second honeymoon or decide to just swing in a hammock for a while and your business will continue to grow.

Some time ago, Linda Litle of Bozeman, Montana, leader of a rapidly growing group, won a trip to Japan through her company. Her husband, a physician, could not leave his practice to accompany her, yet when she returned from her trip her business had doubled because those in her group had been working while she was away. Her husband, meanwhile, had worked long hours just to maintain his patient load.

"That's when my husband said, 'Hey, I'd better look at this,' " Linda said.

THE EXACT FORMULA BY WHICH a Network Marketing company rewards its distributors is called a "compensation plan." Compensation plans vary from company to company. Each includes different requirements and compensation methods, based on the company's products, its philosophy, the customer base it is trying to reach and its vision of the future.

Some plans encourage representatives to build their organizations wide, that is, to sponsor many people directly. Others provide the greatest compensation to those who build depth, who sponsor a few people at a time and then teach them to sponsor others in a similar way throughout the Network.

In addition to commissions based on retail sales and bonuses awarded for group sales, some plans provide additional compensation by increasing the discount on products as you advance through the organization. For instance, according to one compensation plan, you may buy your product from Anna, your sponsor, for 20 percent off retail. You then are able to make an instant 20 percent profit by reselling those products at their retail price.

At the same time, Anna, because she has more people in her group and therefore a higher sales volume, may be eligible to buy her products from Ben, her sponsor, for 30 percent off the retail price. She makes a 10 percent profit on what she sells to you and 30 percent on any products she retails herself. Ben, in turn, may receive 40 percent off his products from Carl, who buys directly from the company for 50 percent off.

In another type of plan, all distributors buy their products at wholesale prices directly from the company, yet as the amount of product moving through their group grows, distributors may become eligible for even deeper discounts.

Don't be deceived by skeptics who say that compensation

plans based on exponential growth are sure to implode under the weight of their own development. It's true that carried to its extreme, the concept of exponential growth would, at least on paper, have everyone in the world signed up as a distributor to some company in short order, leaving no one for those who enter late to sponsor.

That's not going to happen. Not everyone wants to begin a Networking business. The timing may not be right for one or more of a hundred reasons. Some will never be interested in the concept. Others join a company and then drop out when they don't find a way to get rich quick, or a quick-fix solution to whatever problems confront them.

EXPERIENCED NETWORKERS SAY those who begin part-time, who take the time to learn their business and who make a commitment to stick to it, can expect to earn from several hundred to several thousand dollars per month. The opportunity for full-time Networkers is unlimited, depending on the time, energy and skill they bring to their work. Yet no matter what the compensation level, prosperity is more than a bonus check, and Networking offers additional, equally tangible rewards:

• TAX ADVANTAGES. As owner of your own home-based business, you may be eligible for potent tax advantages and retirement savings. Check carefully with your accountant. Many of the costs of doing business are tax deductible, even if the people you are doing business with are family and friends.

• SMALL INITIAL INVESTMENT. You can begin your business with a small initial investment. Today, for example, franchises provide one of the most popular ways to be self-employed.

But franchises can cost from $10,000 to $1 million and inventory and equipment can cost as much again or more.

Most franchise owners begin their new ventures under a load of debt. For their investment, they receive the right to use the name of a well-known company, along with company support and training in a proven method of operation. Those are the very same things you, as owner of your own Network Marketing business, will receive from your company and your sponsor, usually for less than $500.00.

• LOW OVERHEAD. As a Network Marketer, you can begin your business immediately with no overhead, no leases, no employees and no contracts. With no accounts receivable and little or no inventory. Some companies are so sophisticated that all paperwork, even collection and distribution of sales tax, is handled directly from the company. You assume only responsibility for making sure your home-based business meets state and local regulations.

• IMMEDIATE PROFITS. Business consultants say most small start-up businesses should be prepared to lose money for as long as a year, as they build their customer base. You, on the other hand, are poised for immediate success, because you can pay for your own growth out of business profits realized from day one.

And as a business owner, you may find you enjoy greater standing in your community. Small business owners are one of the most powerful segments in today's economy; they are the innovators providing the majority of our nation's employment opportunities.

- FLEXIBLE HOURS. If you're already employed, you can begin your Networking business while retaining your present job. Ninety percent of Network Marketers work their businesses part-time. Many of today's industry leaders began building their businesses with an investment of only a few select hours each week.

In Network Marketing, you are free to fit your work around your life, not your life around your work. You can arrange your business hours so you can be available to your children, your parents and your friends, and you can choose with whom you work, as well. You build your organization to include those who add enjoyment and satisfaction to your life; your customers are people you already care about and those you meet along the way to greater achievement.

Some people find they enjoy their new business so much they simply decide to grow it large enough to allow it to become their primary source of income. Others turn to their Network Marketing business when they lose their regular job. And some decide early to commit to becoming a Network leader. Their dream is to build a significant income, one that allows them total financial security and freedom.

All these business building strategies are possible. The advantage of Network Marketing is that you decide how you want to grow your business. And you decide if and when to change that strategy.

- FAMILY TIME. Your new business may even offer a chance to get to know your family better. "A moonlight business happens to be especially suited for family enterprises, because of the obvious built-in support and mutual assistance afforded by members of the family: a built-in, already functioning combination of interests," writes Philip Holland in *How to Start a Business Without Quitting Your Job.*

"The business will produce not only collective income, but also the opportunity to work in harmony for a common cause. Indeed, the economic interdependence of a family business can become the cohesive remedy for the splintered nature of contemporary family life."

Yet even with all the above tangible advantages, the most powerful reward may be one that comes from within yourself.

As a Network Marketing business owner, you are free to chart your own course to success. You, with guidance and support from your sponsor and company, decide how to build your business. Your time is your own. No boss looks over your shoulder; you punch no time clock.

"Playing the role of entrepreneur can provide a marvelous contrast from the frustrations inherent in salaried jobs," Holland writes. "It will offset the muddy compromises one must wade through when working for others. It will provide the opportunity for self-realization that eludes us at work. The exercise of final authority will revitalize your mental and physical powers and tap into a reservoir of strength unrealized during the absence of opportunity. Being president is exhilarating and can properly be described as the sweetest morsel in the candy store."

5

Of Scoundrels and Visionaries

"Stocks have reached what looks like
a permanently high plateau."
— Irving Fisher, Professor of Economics,
Yale University, Oct. 17, 1929

IF NETWORK MARKETING is such a powerful way to build individual wealth, why aren't the world's business leaders talking more about it? Why haven't we learned about this concept from a professor of economics instead of from our best friend's sister?

That's the magic of Network Marketing.

Remember, companies who choose to distribute their goods and services through Network Marketers don't have to spend millions of dollars on prime time advertisements, Sunday morning "infomercials" or enough direct mailers and magazine ads to doom several national forests. You won't hear about it on television or from professional economists.

Instead, Network Marketing relies on the oldest, most powerful advertising medium ever devised—word of mouth.

Mark tells a business colleague, Sue, about his new part-time venture. Sue becomes intrigued and tells Jan, her doctor. Jan, seeing the success Sue begins to enjoy, becomes involved and tells her brother and her stockbroker. At the end of just that one chain of conversational events, Mark finds himself working with four new business builders, receiving bonuses from all their sales and from all those who follow them. Mark's business grows from one simple conversation with a co-worker.

And just because it's not yet taught at the Harvard Business School, doesn't mean Network Marketing isn't a powerful economic force with its own rich history.

"The concept of using a geometric progression to establish control within an organization, or to pass along information, has been present for centuries," writes Michael Harden, in his industry study, *The Handbook of Multi-Level Marketing*.

"Before the written word, primitive societies would pass legends, stories and other tribal information on to younger members of the tribe. They, in turn, would pass the information on to the next generation. Of course, as this process continued with each generation, new information and stories were added, thereby increasing each generation's knowledge."

THROUGHOUT THE CENTURIES Network Marketing, like all powerful concepts, has evolved. Like all economic systems, it has been molded through the years by geniuses and scoundrels alike, by visionaries and an occasional huckster.

One of the first modern uses of the concept of exponential growth to generate income may have been the chain letter craze that swept the U.S. after World War I. The letters promised great profit if you would just send a dime—or sometimes a dollar—to the person at the top of the list and add your name to the bottom.

The chain letters spread as far as Europe and by the mid-1930s, the U.S. post office estimated that 10 million such letters were being mailed each day—even as postal authorities and law enforcement agencies battled the fraudulent schemes. The chain letter phenomenon began to subside in the early 1940s, although school children and an occasional adult may still receive a version, usually without the unlawful request for money.

Modern Network Marketing is almost 50 years old. Then more commonly known as multi-level marketing, it began in the mid-1940s with the NutraLite Food Supplement Corp. "Like many truly innovative breakthroughs," the development of true Network Marketing was an accident, writes David Stewart, in his book *Network Marketing: An Action Guide for Success*.

NutraLite, a company that offered food supplements, originally was organized as a direct selling company. Independent distributors would buy its products and resell them directly to consumers. Nutralite's products proved to be so popular and beneficial that the company found consumers were recommending them to their friends and becoming distributors "based on their enjoyment of the product's benefits and a desire for additional income. That was a far cry from the cold-calling on strangers, hype and high-pressure techniques employed by door-to-door and conventional sales," Stewart writes.

In 1943, NutraLite restructured its marketing program to encourage each of its distributors to build—and be compensated for—their own individual sales organizations. Distributors were to receive bonuses on product sales made by those they sponsored, through a certain number of levels.

In 1956, NutraLite was joined in Network Marketing by Dr. Forrest Shaklee, who founded the Shaklee company to gain wider distribution of the food supplements he had developed in his clinic. Over the years, Shaklee would grow to include more than a million North American distributors who offer almost 150 products.

Not long after, in 1959, former NutraLite distributors Rich DeVos and Jay Van Andel drew on the words "American" and "way" to name their own new personal and household products company Amway. Shaklee and Amway, two of Network Marketing's true pioneers, paved the way for a new form of business.

Unfortunately, that pavement proved slippery for a handful of scoundrels more interested in getting rich quick than in operating legitimate businesses.

As entrepreneurs rushed to adopt this new form of distribution, some overstepped the bounds of ethical business practices. Mutated forms of multi-level marketing turned into schemes designed to reward distributors solely for signing up others, not for marketing legitimate products. Some companies forced distributors to pay huge up-front fees or hidden charges for questionable reasons. Other fast-talkers entered the arena, reaped quick sign-up fees and then disappeared. These schemes came to be known as "pyramids," because they often rewarded those first enticed into the organization, to the detriment of those who joined later.

In 1974, Sen. Walter Mondale declared such companies to be the nation's number one consumer fraud. Companies such as Koscot Interplanetary, Holiday Magic and Bestline Products were shut down by government regulators.

Law enforcement agencies moved quickly to clean up the

abuses. In the mid-1970s, burned by illegitimate schemes and scoundrels—and with still no clear idea of what constituted a legitimate use of multi-level marketing—the Federal Trade Commission and state agencies across the nation turned their wary eyes on almost all multi-level companies. In 1975, the FTC filed suit against Amway, alleging that the company was an illegal pyramid and that its refusal to sell its products in retail stores constituted a restraint of trade.

Amway spent four years and millions of dollars in legal fees to clear its name. In 1979, the FTC ruled that Amway was not a pyramid, that it did in fact generate substantial revenue from the sale of its products to consumers. In addition, the FTC acknowledged that Amway had "built a substantial manufacturing company and an efficient distribution system," according to Michael Harden's account of the settlement.

Amway and other multi-level companies that fought to prove their legitimacy won important victories for Network Marketing. And Network Marketing exploded in the next decade, as companies entered the newly vindicated industry . . .

"Every industry goes through an evolution," says Kelly Thayer, who in 1993 was named *Inc.* magazine's Entrepreneur of the Year. Thayer and his company, Clear Image, Inc., produce presentation videos for many of the top U.S. Network Marketing companies.

"In the 1960s as franchising was emerging, it was looked on as a scam, yet today more than 60 percent of all businesses are franchises," Thayer says. "Chiropractors were called the quacks of the 1970s. And look at the stock market; in the early days, the stock market was considered shady. All concepts run their course; they work the bugs out. In the decade of the 90s, you will see Network Marketing become the preferred way of marketing products."

The struggles in the early years of Network Marketing made important contributions to its future. They defined the ethics and standards by which the Network Marketing industry governs itself today. Government and industry officials continue to keep a close eye on questionable ventures that seem to search out the law's gray areas or look for loopholes in today's ethics and standards. That increase in credibility is one reason for Network Marketing's growth.

"Today we're seeing a change in the types of people attracted to this industry," says attorney Hugh Clemmons, Jr. "They demand more ethics and professionalism from the companies and they're refusing to do business with companies that don't live up to those expectations."

Network Marketing has evolved in other ways, as well.

Many of today's Network companies began as direct selling companies, in which independent distributors sold primarily to a large number of retail customers. Examples include Avon Products Inc., Watkins Products, and Encyclopedia Britannica North America. In the last few years, however, many direct selling companies have switched to Network Marketing.

They found they still were able to get their products directly to their customers but without the dreaded "s-" word, because, when asked, more than 95 percent of people will say either that they *can't* sell or they *hate* to sell.

Because Network Marketers build their Networks of customers from among those they already know or those they meet as they go about their activities—that word-of-mouth concept, again—they do not have to make "cold-calls" on strangers. They sponsor only those who may be interested and then teach them to continue the process.

One other reason for the decline of direct selling is that, beginning in the 1970s and continuing today, when distributors made those cold calls, no one was home. Women, long the customer backbone of direct sales, had entered the workforce in astounding numbers, leaving few behind to buy spices and encyclopedias and cosmetics.

Even companies who emphasized party plans, in which a "hostess" would gather a few of her friends for a presentation by an independent distributor, suffered. After a day at work, few women had the time or inclination to venture out again in the evening, even for what was usually billed as a social evening with friends.

Companies watching these societal trends moved quickly to revise their compensation plans to allow for other, more informal, methods of sale. According to the DSA, in 1995 only 32.1 percent of sales took place in a party or group setting. More than 64.9 percent of 1995 sales were from one individual to another, one-to-one.

Although 59 percent of 1995 sales were transacted in the home, it most likely was on a more informal basis rather that a traditional sales call. And the percentage of sales taking place in the workplace has grown from 11.7 percent in 1988 to almost 15 percent in 1995.

NETWORK MARKETING HAS GROWN in the years since the 1979 Amway vindication, in both size and stature. Today's companies represent products and services that include those on the forefront of innovation and imagination, products that often are not available anywhere else. Network Marketers are leading the way with healthful, natural and earth-friendly products,

products that today are bringing us healthier and more reward-
ing lives.

Millions of independent businessmen and women are representing their companies with integrity and grace. And they're
reaping the rewards.

6

Your Graduate Education

"Winning is in understanding the rules and
knowing how the game is played."
— Michael S. Clouse

*Susan Edison pushed herself back from the computer console in
her office and laughed out loud—both at herself and at the vision of
her friend Geoffrey on the screen in front of her.*

Geoffrey grinned back at her.

*"There's no way I'm going to make it to the Cape by Friday," he
said. "My in-basket is leaning like the Tower of Pisa. I could be crushed
at any moment. We'll be lucky if we make it by Sunday afternoon.
How long are you staying? Theresa and I need to get back by the
15th. We're starting a new group in New Orleans and I promised to
set up training sessions there by the end of the month."*

*"No problem," Susan said. "The kids and I are coming out on
Tuesday, but Tom won't make it until the weekend. We're going to
stay for a few weeks. As long as I have a power source, I can keep in
touch as well there as here."*

*"Great," Geoffrey said. "We'll get a chance for a real visit. I'll get
started on this list of ideas and beam you a progress report tomorrow.*

"Hey, and give Andy a call, would you? He says Samantha has

big news." With a wave, Geoffrey disappeared from the screen.

Susan laughed again. What a pair.

She never would have guessed Geoffrey and Andy would become such good friends. They were so very different . . .

Geoffrey was her banker when she had first started her business. He was a shrewd businessman, and he had watched the bank mergers and consolidations of the 1990s with a wary eye. When his community bank was bought out by a financial corporation in 1995, he took advantage of the bank's early retirement offer to its middle management. As he had brainstormed new career ideas, he remembered Susan's success and gave her a call to talk about the opportunities in Network Marketing.

Geoffrey had been a fast starter.

He had used his ability to read people, his firsthand knowledge of their worries about financial insecurity and a high energy level to spread the word about his company's products and opportunities. Before the end of his second year in business, he had matched his former bank salary, and by the end of his third year, he had doubled it. Today, he not only earned enough to insure his family's future, he also had the free time to enjoy being with them now . . .

But Andy!

Andy had joined Susan about the same time as Geoffrey. He had been a young man with a good, steady job. When he talked with Susan he told her he and his wife, Samantha, were looking for a second income, something that would allow them to provide their young children with a few of the extras in life. The trouble was, between their jobs, the children and Andy's elderly parents, neither had much time to devote to any additional venture.

Even so, together with Susan they had mapped out a few extra hours a week. Susan assured them that many people are able to build substantial part-time businesses in Network Marketing by commit-

ting only five or 10 or 15 hours a week (see Appendix B).

Andy and Samantha took her at her word and went to work.

They told their friends, their family and their co-workers about their new business and introduced them to their company's products. When their friends and family found they could substitute the products they were now using with ones of higher quality—and discovered they would be delivered directly to their door—some began to buy from Andy and Samantha at retail prices. That meant an immediate profit for their fledgling business.

Others, after trying some of the products, decided they wanted to buy them at wholesale prices directly from the company. That saved them money and earned Andy and Samantha a bonus every time someone placed an order.

One by one, over time, those they introduced to their company told others about the products and opportunities. As new people joined, Andy and Samantha's group grew. And so did their monthly bonus checks.

Neither of them quit their jobs. They didn't take out a loan to pay for business start-up costs. And they sure didn't have to leave their children with baby sitters to build their business. They simply told the people they knew—and those they met as they went about their day—about their company and its products. Some were interested enough to try the products. Others weren't. Some wanted to know more about the new business. Others never asked for more information.

Andy and Samantha didn't get rich quick. But by the time they had worked at their new business for a few months, they knew they were making progress toward their goals. They enjoyed sharing their discovery with those they knew. And although their bonus checks were small, they knew they were building the foundation for their future success.

Then something began to happen.

Samantha's Uncle Paul in Detroit bought one of the products. He introduced it to his buddies at work, who told their relatives, and suddenly Andy and Samantha had a hot group growing in Detroit. A couple of months later, Andy's sister's best friend in Baton Rouge lost her job and decided to take her part-time Network Marketing business more seriously. By the end of the year, she was head of one of the fastest growing groups in the company and Andy and Samantha were shopping for tax shelters.

Now, eight years later, Geoffrey and Andy are golfing buddies with plans to start a snorkeling equipment company in the Bahamas, just for fun. They are two of Susan's top associates, yet each chose a different path to get them there.

Geoffrey started out fast, and his success seemed to come just as rapidly.

Andy and Samantha, with help from Susan and their company, built their business at their own slow and steady pace. They took time along the way to watch their children grow and to care for Andy's mother. Even so, only a few years later, their business provided them with much more than the extras they had first hoped for. It allowed them a life they had only dreamed of before. All by working a few consistent extra hours a week with family, with friends and with friends of friends.

N O TWO NETWORK MARKETING COMPANIES are alike. Compensation plans differ, as do products and business philosophies. Each company has a different personality and a different focus. Some extremely reputable companies are flamboyant, others are more businesslike. Each approaches its product development, its distributor community and its business decisions a little differently.

48

Even so, top-class Network companies share several important characteristics. They adhere to the industry's highest principles and codes of ethics *(see Appendix C)*. They value their distributor community and they constantly look for ways to improve both their services and their products.

If you choose to become a Network business owner, your choice of company will be one of your most important decisions. Look for:

1. COMPANY EXPERIENCE IN NETWORK MARKETING.

Other business experience is good, but you are looking for experience in Network Marketing. Network Marketing is an alternate method of product distribution. It also is a very different way to structure a company. Make sure the company you select has been in business long enough to prove it knows what it's doing. Many of the here-today, gone-tomorrow companies that fly through the Network Marketing community simply didn't know what they were getting into.

2. LENGTH OF TIME IN BUSINESS.

There's a philosophy in Network Marketing that says if you get in on the ground floor of a hot new company, you'll rise to the top as it grows. Perhaps. But for every true opportunity, there are at least a dozen companies that come on strong, then fizzle and fade, leaving their distributors with downlines, but no company. Many experienced Networkers feel it may be better to catch the elevator on the second or third floor and ride the rest of the way to the top.

On the other hand, some of today's most exciting companies, even though they're young, are on the forefront of the Network Marketing revolution. Experienced industry leaders are putting together new companies that offer the best of the old with the innovations of the new.

If the company you are considering is young, don't pass it up. Just take one more look. Make sure it is prepared to handle the rapid growth that may lie ahead and make sure it meets our other criteria.

3. STRONG FINANCIAL BASE.

More companies in all types of business fail because of lack of financial depth than all other reasons put together. Network Marketing companies, especially young ones, are under particular stress. They can grow rapidly, straining their ability to finance their growth responsibly. It takes a steady management hand on the wheel to chart a course between the rapid growth of Networking and a solid balance sheet for the future.

4. TOP-FLIGHT COMPANY MANAGEMENT AND PROFES-SIONALISM.

You want that hand at the wheel to know which way it needs to steer. You want your company's management to be experienced, inventive, creative and professional.

Check to see if the company you are considering is a member of an industry association such as the Direct Selling Association or the Multi-level Marketing International Association. For example, many of Network Marketing's top companies belong to the DSA. Those who join undergo close scrutiny and a membership waiting period, and they agree to adhere to the association's strict code of ethics.

5. COMPANY COMMITMENT TO ITS DISTRIBUTORS.

The company you want to work for values its distributors.

It is constantly looking for ways to improve its products, the way it does business and its ability to help you do your job and build your business. It knows what you need and helps you in that regard.

Quality companies know their success depends on your success and they're there, offering training, support, education and encouragement. You need to know that your company is committed to your success and to its future as a Network Marketing company.

6. PROFESSIONAL-QUALITY PRESENTATION TOOLS.

"I've found the business opportunity of a lifetime," a friend tells you. "You've *got* to take a look at this. Easy Street, here I come." Then he hands you a faded and crinkled copy of a copy of a copy. What are the chances you'll take him seriously?

Before you sign on any enrollment agreement line, make sure your company has the tools you will need to make your business a success. Tools like business cards and professional-looking and informative product catalogs and brochures. Perhaps a company presentation video and a distributor training program.

Once you know your company has them, use them. Nothing squelches a business opportunity faster than finding yourself with someone who wants to know more about your business just as you remember you gave your last brochure to your brother-in-law.

7. PRODUCTS PEOPLE WILL WANT TO BUY.

Your company's products don't need to be proprietary; giant Network Marketing companies have made billions of dollars by selling laundry detergent and cosmetics. Just make sure

51

the Network company you choose offers products people want to buy, either because they are an exceptional value, they're of exceptional quality or because they offer exceptional service and convenience. Whether it's food supplements, long distance services or satellite systems, your customers must already use or really want what you have to offer.

8. EMPHASIS ON PRODUCTS.

Legitimate Networking companies compensate their distributors for sales, not for sponsoring others. Their compensation plans are based on making sure the company's products get to the end consumers, whether retail or wholesale.

Distributor enrollment fees are reasonable, usually under $100. Legitimate companies do not require a large investment in inventory, known as front-loading. And they offer a liberal buy-back policy for any unsold inventory.

In addition, look for a company that offers your customers a money-back guarantee on products they purchase through you.

9. ROOM TO GROW.

Brand new companies offer plenty of room to grow, but they also offer a greater degree of risk. Carefully evaluate the level of risk you want to assume in your new business.

Do not automatically rule out companies who already have a strong market presence. Some very large and very successful companies already have tens of thousands of distributors, yet those who join still find success. There's no denying it may take more time and effort to build a large organization with a company that already has established a substantial presence in an area. That's why some Networkers prefer to join a company that still has plenty of room to grow.

But remember, in Network Marketing, you are building your business by introducing your products to those you know. Even if most of the rest of the world already uses your company's products, your friends and family may not and you can still build a business by sharing your products and business success with them.

10. DISTRIBUTOR SUPPORT.

Networking is a simple business, but it's not easy. Those at the top already know what works and what doesn't. There are keys to success in Networking, just as there are in any endeavor.

As a beginner, you may not know all those keys—yet, but that's okay. Make sure the sponsor and the company you choose are committed to helping you learn them.

Strong support from your company's product knowledge department, marketing department and area coordinators can mean the difference between success and disappointment.

Strong support from your sponsor, as well as their sponsor and their sponsor's sponsor, are vital to reaching the level of achievement you have chosen. Before you join a company, ask how much help you can expect from those above you in your organization.

11. A PRODUCT YOU LOVE.

In your career as a Networker, nothing will make your life simpler or more enjoyable than a catalog full of products or services you believe in. If you use and enjoy your company's products—and you must, for success—you won't be able to keep yourself from recommending them to those you know.

Remember the last time you saw a movie you particularly

enjoyed? Chances are the next day at work you recommended it to your co-workers. They may have gone to see the movie on your recommendation and taken a friend or spouse along with them. If they liked it, they may even have recommended it to others, who then also went to see the film. That's how movies turn into box office smashes.

Well, what if you received a check from the theater for each person you or your friends referred? It would be a pleasant extra income, but you would have recommended the movie anyway, because you sincerely thought it provided a good evening's entertainment. Your company's products should play the same role.

You want to choose a company whose products you would use even if you did not market them or receive any compensation from their sale. Then your enthusiasm for them will spill over onto other's efforts and benefit everyone involved.

12. A SENSE OF FUN.

One additional—and not entirely lighthearted piece of advice: find a company that's fun. Find one that inspires you to greater heights of creativity, one that attracts positive and joyful people, the kind you'll look forward to spending time with. Many of the people in your company will become your closest associates and dearest friends. Make sure they add beauty and quality and integrity to your life, as well as income to your pocketbook.

AS YOU BEGIN YOUR NEW BUSINESS, you will want the best training you can get to make sure you have the greatest possible chance for success. Imagine that tomorrow when you arrive at the office, your boss calls you in and presents you with an offer like this one:

"We like what you're doing here. We think you have a great future with this company. We see a period of strong growth ahead, so we've decided to invest in one of our most valuable assets—you.

"We'd like you to go back to school to get that advanced management degree you've talked about. We'll pay for the education. You can schedule your classes after work and on weekends. It probably will take you less than two years. When you've completed your work, we will immediately raise your salary by $1,500 a month. And you'll have an education that will benefit you the rest of your career. All you need to do is invest some of your spare time. Are you interested?"

Believe it or not, many—maybe even most—of those presented with this opportunity would say, "No." Change is difficult and habits, even habits like watching television every evening, feel familiar and are difficult to break.

Yet when successful Network Marketers, as entrepreneurs, begin their business, they accept an offer much like this one—whether they know it or not. They choose to take some of their free time and invest it in their future. They make a commitment to study with those more experienced in their field in order to increase their skills, and they put what they learn to immediate use in their business.

Students enrolled in a graduate-level course on Network Marketing would learn the newest approaches to the basics of the business. They would learn how to duplicate what they learn, so that all others in their group could share their success and they would practice ways to use their new skills on the job.

Let's listen in. First, the basics.

THERE IS ONLY ONE SUREFIRE WAY to build a solid Networking business. It requires no selling and no persuasion, and anyone can do it. There are other bells and whistles and fancy fender flairs available—they're next—but this basic model will take you anywhere you want to go:

1. **Use your company's products and services.**

Whatever your company makes that you can use, use it. If it's a product, don't wait until you run out of what you have on hand. Using all your company's products sets a good example for those who may join you in the business. You never know when the practice may lead to new business.

Imagine one Networker's embarrassment when a friend admired her new gold bracelet. If she had been wearing one of her company's bracelets, she might have won herself a new customer.

2. **Each month, buy the amount of inventory your company requires to remain active.**

Buy it, as we say in Network Marketing, "to use, to share and to show." Use your company's products or services at home, give them as gifts, have them available to prospective customers and build enough inventory to demonstrate products to those you sponsor.

3. **Find five people and teach them to do the same.**

That's all there is to it. Then help your people find and teach *their* people.

That's it.

As you establish your business, your sponsor will teach you how to most effectively put the fundamentals into practice, as well as the latest techniques to help you build your business in the most efficient way. To speed you on your way, we offer a few additional ideas for rapidly building a vibrant business:

1.   Tell your friends, your family and your co-workers about your new business, of course.

2.   List everyone you know.
Everyone knows several hundred people. Get their names down on paper. You don't need to call them all now, but write down as many names as you can—your plumber, your veterinarian, your sister's best friend. As names come to you, whether in the middle of the night or during dinner or while you're watching a movie, jot them down and then add them to your list. Your goal is to make a list of everyone you know by name and then to add to the list as you meet new people.

Review the list often and think about how what you are offering could be of value to the friends you find there. Does someone have dry skin? Perhaps your company offers an effective moisturizer. Is another friend on the list under stress at work? Perhaps one of your nutritional supplements would help provide relief. Would your oil additive protect the engine of your neighbor's new car? Perhaps your weight loss system is just the ticket for the co-worker who mentioned he would like to lose a few pounds.

Perhaps someone on the list is worried about not having enough money or is concerned about losing contact with their teens. A Networking business can make a terrific family project, especially when everyone knows the additional income will go toward a joint family goal.

3. Don't prejudge whether someone may be interested in what you have to offer.

Even millionaires may be looking for an opportunity that offers a growing income with less effort or stress. Doctors' incomes, as we mentioned earlier, rely solely on their time with patients, and they tend to have to work long stressful hours to pay for their costs of doing business. Many would welcome a part-time business that allows them to multiply their efforts by combining them with others. Stockbrokers, bankers, physicians, artists, captains of industry—all have built successful Networking businesses. In fact, those who are successful in one field often are more able to envision success in another.

Yet don't rule out those who are still struggling to find their place in life. Just as many people who are unemployed, undereducated or hard-pressed have risen to find great success in Network Marketing.

4. Put your sponsor to work for you.

If you decide you would like to grow your business, the best way to do that as a beginner is to find people for your sponsor to talk to. Tell those you know about your new venture, then invite anyone who asks to know more about your products or about the business opportunity to speak with your sponsor:

"You're right, Alex. I am excited. This is a quality company. And it's a great chance to own my own business. The potential is there for a significant income. And I have to tell you, I'm new at this. I'm still learning the ropes myself . . .

"Tell you what, I'm having coffee with my sponsor tomorrow night. Why don't I stop by and pick you up? I'll probably only have

about half-an-hour with him, but you'll enjoy meeting Tom, and he'll be able to answer some of those questions."

5. Put the printed word to work for you.

Send a press release announcing the opening of your business to your local newspaper. Don't forget any specialty business publications in your area.

And pass out your business cards. Go through them as fast as you can. Leave them with your tip as you leave a restaurant. Stick them on bulletin boards and include a couple any time you pay a bill.

Some Networkers place advertisements in newspapers and trade journals, looking for others who may want to join them in their business. In there training materials, Randy Gage and Tom Schreiter both offer excellent guides to using advertising media. We tell you how to obtain them in Appendix A.

6. Practice a couple of easy ice breakers.

Ice breakers allow you to meet people and give you a natural way to talk about your business. For instance, think of how many times you have waited in line to buy a ticket for a movie. Perhaps it is your habit to strike up a conversation with the person in front of you and chat for a moment about the weather or current events.

During a natural pause in the conversation, it's very easy to pull out your business card, smile warmly and say:

"You're an easy person to talk with. May I give you my card? You know, I'm always looking for people just like you to work with me in my business. I have no idea if you would be interested in what we're doing, but if you keep your business options

open, I would like to discuss this with you in more detail. Please, feel free to give me a call any time."

Then change the subject. You don't need to mention it again. If they're interested or curious, they'll ask you more, and as you gain experience you will become comfortable talking more directly about your business.

7. Use audio and video information kits.

One of the most exciting developments in Networking has taken place in just the last few years, with the development of audio tapes and videos that tell about Network Marketing or present a company, its products or services, and its business opportunity. The use of these information kits can quickly and dramatically multiply your own business-building efforts.

Information kits do two things: They move products and sponsor distributors. A study by the Wharton School of Business showed that video brochures increased retention by almost 50 percent and expedited buying decisions by as much as 72 percent, compared to print advertising. And the study also found that three times as many people were likely to request a video as ask for printed information. And they were six times more likely to respond to an offer made in a video brochure than to a printed ad.

Audio and video information kits can be used both locally and long distance as a screening tool. They can help you find those who want to know more about your products or business. Time is money, and information kits are one way to leverage both.

Typically, a Networker builds a number of different kits. Each may contain an audio tape that tells about the benefits of

Network Marketing, an interesting, easy-to-read book (*Future Choice* is one example) that explains how Network Marketing works, or perhaps a short video tape. Networkers simply loan the information kit to someone they know, then return in a day or two to pick it up and answer any questions they may have.

Again, let's look at this technique through the doubling concept.

If, as your business grows, you have 10 distributors, each with 10 information kits, that means that at any given time there is the potential for 100 presentations being made. One hundred distributors with 10 kits means the potential for 1,000 presentations, each given exactly the same way.

Do you see how this approach allows you to leverage your effort many times over?

Even if you decide to take a day off, you will know that your representatives, through information kits, are giving professional presentations to hundreds of potential business builders or customers. Audio tapes, video tapes and books are particularly effective because they never have a bad day; they are never more excited or more complacent one time than another. They tell the story exactly the same way, every time. They present a true ability to duplicate your message with those you contact and they allow you to quickly reach many people.

If you choose to rapidly build your business, experienced Networkers recommend you pass out at least one information kit six days a week. Two days after you loan out the first kit, return to pick it up. Answer any questions, and then pass it on to someone else. The next day, pick up the second kit and do the same thing. You will be contacting 12 people a week—those you gave the kits to last week and those they're going to this week.

One comfortable way to pass out information kits or other material about your company is called a third-party referral system: You simply ask those you know to refer you to someone else who might be interested in what your company has to offer. When you talk with that person, mention who made the referral. If you were to make contact by telephone, the conversation could go like this:

> *"Jan, my name is John Smith. Sandy Nelson and I were visiting yesterday and she suggested I give you a call. My wife and I have just started a new business and we're looking for a few sharp people to work with us. Sandy spoke very highly of you and mentioned you might be exactly what we're looking for. I'm curious, are you open to any offers?"*

Jan is sure to want to know more! Even if it turns out that she is not interested, she may know someone who is. A variation to the third-party referral offers the chance to obtain even more contacts.

> *"Jan, my name is John Smith. Sandy Nelson suggested that I give you a call. My wife and I have just started a new business and Sandy thought you might know of someone who is looking for a substantial second income. Jan, who do you know that might be interested in earning an extra $500 to $2,000 per month?"*

8. Avoid a hard-sell approach.

Each of our suggested business-builder ideas relies on an easy and natural way of talking with people. That's important.

Because, hard sell went out of style in the 1980s.

Today's consumers and potential distributors are more sophisticated. No one wants to be browbeaten, even with the financial opportunity of a lifetime. Sharp Networkers inform people of what they're doing, let them know they would like to do business with them and then keep in touch, lightly. They look for ways to offer value and they let people know they respect their ability to make decisions that are right for them at any given time.

THE ONLY ADDITIONAL KEY to any successful Network Marketing venture is to find what works and repeat it. Repeat it again, and then teach those you sponsor to repeat it. It's a concept known in the business as "being duplicatable."

All efforts in Networking are measured by whether they can be easily and correctly duplicated. As author and noted success trainer Tony Robbins teaches, success leaves clues. Just find and emulate someone who has achieved the level of success you desire.

You don't have to figure out Network Marketing on your own. You can select a company that already is enjoying a high level of success. And you can choose with whom to work from any number of talented people in your upline. It's not like going to work for IBM. In the traditional corporate world, you can't decide which company you want to represent, then walk in, find out who is the nicest boss and request to work only with them.

But you can in Network Marketing. After you have been sponsored, you can go "upline" and speak to your sponsor's sponsor, and to their sponsor, and to their sponsor, until you find the person that you feel comfortable with. You can interview these leaders and even select one to be your personal mentor. If they are the type of leader you are looking for, they will be pleased to work with you.

In addition to working personally with your own mentor, each company contains top groups whose members can offer many valuable insights. And leaders in the Network Marketing industry itself have authored many excellent guides to success. Some of the best are listed in the back of this book. Your company's training system, combined with those available from these professional Network trainers, will quickly get you started on your advanced degree. With them, you have available to you proven methods for success from the first minute you open your business.

7
Challenges and Choices

"Jonathan Livingston Seagull will never
make it as a paperback."
— James Galton, publisher, refusing an offer
by MacMillan Company to bid on paperback
rights for Richard Bach's best-selling novel.
Ten years later, paperback sales reached
more than 7 million copies.

I T'S GOING TO HAPPEN, so you may as well plan for it. It
could be your sister, your mother or your best friend, your
racquetball partner or your golf caddie. You're going to go
to someone whose opinion you value, brimming with excite-
ment about your new business. Before you're even halfway fin-
ished describing it, they will look at you and say, with the same
tone of voice they use to discuss the Internal Revenue Service,
"This sounds like one of those pyramid schemes."

And then their mind will snap shut. You'll be able to hear it
clang closed; nothing you will be able to say will make a difference. It happens to everyone.

Some people just don't want to hear about Network Marketing. Ever. Even if they love you and would ordinarily sup-

port you in any way they could. Some people are just suspicious of the unfamiliar. Or maybe they've been hit by one too many hard-sells. Maybe they know someone who has had a bad experience with multi-level marketing. Perhaps they themselves at one time chose a bad company or suffered through a bad sponsor. Either way, they may have ended up with a garage full of products, a credit card full of charges and an address book full of former friends.

Ouch.

Luckily, if you choose to become involved in Network Marketing, most of those you approach with your new venture will be delighted at your enthusiasm and open to what you have to present. But if you find yourself hurt when someone you care about doesn't seem happy for you, take a deep breath and then take a second look at their reaction.

They are concerned for you. They may be leery that you're going to pester them to buy things they don't want or to join a company they don't care about.

Even success can be threatening; they may fear you will change and grow away from them. They may even assume that everyone else shares their opinion about Network Marketing and urge you to drop the idea. All of those things are okay.

Over time, they'll see that although you talk about your work with enthusiasm, you let them decide at what level they want to be involved. They will see that your business adds to your life. It doesn't take you away from theirs.

"I made it a point early on that my close friends and family would have to *ask* to buy from me," says one beginning Networker. "And now they do."

Sooner or later, those who were skeptical *will* ask to try a product or two and before you know it, some of those family members will become your biggest boosters.

Until then, believe it or not, no one *has* to share your enthusiasm for your business. Although it is ideal to have the wholehearted support of your spouse, your family and your friends from the beginning, it's not required. Many Networking fortunes have been built over others' objections, yet by the time those fortunes were well under way, most doubters had long before climbed on board.

Not every one will want to buy your products, and not every one will want to join your company. But plenty will. Your job is to find the ones that do.

How?

By sorting.

PERHAPS ONE OF THE OLDEST Network Marketing stereotypes is that Networkers try to trick people into doing business with them or that they berate friends and family into buying their products.

How unproductive and unprofessional.

Today's Networkers stress the word Networking. They seek to build long-term business relationships based on respect and integrity. They do business with associates in a way that is mutually beneficial by offering valuable goods and services to a growing and willing marketplace. As they prosper, they are able to offer their business opportunity as an exciting possibility for others. Perhaps more than anything else, they demonstrate that Networking is convenient and pleasant.

To find their markets, good Networkers "sort" through people.

They speak openly and joyfully about their company, their products and their business. When appropriate, they offer to share their information and enthusiasm with others. They never try to convince anyone, and they never take rejection personally.

"You never know why someone says 'No,' " says one experienced business-builder. "Maybe it's not the right time for them. Maybe they're feeling stressed. Maybe they had a bad breakfast. Just remember, a 'No' doesn't necessarily mean no. It can mean, 'maybe later.'

"Rejections happen to all of us. If you're not getting rejections, you're not working your business. When it happens to me, I just make a note of the conversation and move on. They're not saying 'No' to me, they're saying 'No' to this opportunity for right now."

One Seattle salesperson agrees, with a witty twist.

His designer auto license plates read, "SWSWSW." Puzzled, we one day got the chance to ask him what the letters meant.

"I'm a salesperson," he says. "I sell for a living. And every time I approach my car, those license plates remind me of the saying I have adopted as my words to live by. The letters stand for, 'Some Will, Some Won't, So What!' "

Indeed!

As Network Marketers build their businesses, some will choose to join. Others won't. So what!

MODERN NETWORK MARKETING CAN OFFER new business owners the training and education they need to make their businesses a success. It also can offer advice that will help newcomers avoid the disappointment and defeat too many earlier Networkers experienced. In general, inexperienced Network Marketers make one common mistake.

Nine out of 10 people who feel they have failed at Network

Marketing believe the company, the product or the concept just doesn't work. They hear about the industry's superstars, the ones who ended their first year in the business with $100,000 of income and a stable of silver BMWs. After a few weeks or months, when they don't see the same results in their own business, too many get discouraged and quit.

Hear us, now.

There are only two basic elements to success in Networking—dedication and persistence. People who fail at Network Marketing stumble for only one reason: they quit too soon.

When that happens, success doesn't bypass their group. It just bypasses them.

Think for a moment about a new attorney setting up a first practice. Would you counsel that attorney to consider the beginning of that business from the day he or she accepted the first case or from the day they entered law school? Probably you would suggest that they count the beginning of their business from the day they actually began to practice law, after completion of their education.

Yet new Networkers too often start counting how long they have been in business from the day they sign on with a company, even if they have no prior experience in Network Marketing. They are too hard on themselves; they allow no time for education. Then, if their new business doesn't yield a significant profit immediately, they get discouraged. They end up looking for the rewards of an advanced degree when they're only halfway through the undergraduate program.

Remember our fictitious friends, Andy and Samantha? At the end of their first year in Networking, they had few distributors, little sales volume and no business builders in sight. But they continued their work.

69

One year later, they were working with Samantha's Uncle Mike and a growing group in Detroit. Before long, they had been joined by Andy's sister's friend, Janet, who quickly developed her own group. Within three years, their struggling little venture had evolved into a prosperous and growing business enterprise.

Tom Schreiter, a top national Networker known for his series of "Big Al" training books, tells a similar story.

Tom and his wife became Networkers when Tom was in his early 20s. Without the training tools available to Networkers today, they managed to make about every mistake possible. After almost two years, they had no distributors, no sales volume and few prospects for the future. But that didn't stop them.

"We didn't know we could quit," Tom says, laughing at his own story. "Our sponsor didn't tell us we had that option." He and his wife continued to work at their business and today Tom Schreiter is one of Networking's superstars. He has reached his goals and fulfilled his dreams, all because he didn't give up.

As a beginning Network Marketer, you will do a lot of things that you do not immediately get paid for. But as your business grows, there will come a day when you will be paid for a lot of things you do not do. That's what makes Network Marketing different from working for someone else. When you have a job, you exchange your time for your employer's money. In Network Marketing, you exchange time up front for a substantial income later.

8

Success Does Leave Clues

"Whether you think you can or you
think you can't, you're right."
— Henry Ford

MEET RANDY GAGE, Jan Ruhe, Dean and Priscilla
Smith, and Tom Schreiter. All five of these entrepreneurs have built large, successful Network Marketing businesses, but they may best be known for how skill-
fully they pass along to others what they have learned. Their
commitment is to teach others how to achieve as they have.
If success does leave clues, these five have many of the answers.

RANDY GAGE:

On most mornings, Network Marketing trainer Randy Gage
walks right past his office to grab his bicycle and pedal out into
another brilliant Florida morning.

With the ocean on his left and the art deco architecture of
Miami Beach on his right, 37-year-old Gage knows his lifestyle
is a powerful advertisement for the business system he teaches.

Gage lives on a small island between Miami and Miami

Beach. His home and his office are in the same building, and while most of us are commuting to work, Gage is bicycling Miami Beach's famous Ocean Drive. And even when he is at work, he is traveling the country teaching the business-building strategies that made him one of the top Network Marketers in the country.

Gage's engaging presentations are known nationwide through his seminars and his best-selling audio tape series, *"How to Earn At Least $100,00 a Year in Network Marketing."* His warm and inspiring audio tape, *"Escape the Rat Race,"* is one of the most potent explanations of Networking's benefits available today.

Gage is at the forefront of those who are bringing Network Marketing into the business world by bringing 21st century communication systems to Networkers. "If you want to be competitive in the 1990s," says Gage, "you'll be using technology. Today's top leaders use e-mail, fax-on-demand, nationwide conference calls, voice information systems . . ."

To all his projects, Gage offers a sly humor and an obvious relish for his work. His message: Today's leaders are using tomorrow's technology, and you can too.

Gage is a top example of how Network Marketing is changing as it emerges into mainstream business circles. Thanks to teachers like Gage, today's Networkers are trained, motivated and professional. In their businesses, they're using many of the business-building techniques practiced by any high technology entrepreneur or Fortune 500 company. They've learned that voice mail boxes, the internet, automated e-mail systems and fax-on-demand services make information—and Networkers—available 24-hours a day without interfering with the lifestyle Networkers cherish.

Yet although Gage is now living the life Networkers strive for, he attained his goals exactly the way he teaches others to reach theirs: he earned them.

"I always say, if I can make it in this business, anyone can," he says. Gage, a Wisconsin native, left home at age 15, a high school drop-out.

"I was a problem, problem child," he says. "I had a real attitude. School, to me, was just the most boring thing."

In his first few years on his own, Gage lied about his age and worked two jobs, both of them for national restaurant chains. "I got excited about the restaurant business," he says. He was made an assistant manager at Howard Johnson's at age 16, although the restaurant thought he was older. He made manager one year later.

"There I was, running a $1 million operation at 17," he says.

Gage became Howard Johnson's problem solver. In five years, he moved to 18 cities, taking over problem stores, turning them around, then moving on to the next challenge. Eventually, he opened his own restaurant and a restaurant consulting business.

Along the way, a friend introduced him to Network Marketing.

"Man, that was it," he says. "To me, it was made just for me. I knew it was perfect."

And how did the future premier trainer do as a Networking beginner?

"*Horrible.* I didn't make a dime. I didn't make *any* money for the first five or six years in the business. I tried other companies, became an MLM junkie. Little by little, I developed my system. I'm not a sales type; I'm a very introverted person. I just kept experimenting and finding what worked. Then I spent another three or four years perfecting the system and another year putting the information together.

"I started a supervisor's school for my own group. I scheduled it for the last Saturday of the month. Other groups heard about it and began to ask to sit in.

"Then somebody flew in from New York for the training, and that just blew me away. Then someone flew in from California—whoa! Then I got invited to take the seminar to Chicago, then New York . . .

"I never looked back. Teaching has always been my favorite part of the business."

Along the way, Gage incorporated personal development techniques into his own life and into his training sessions.

"At some point, I began to set aside personal time every day," he says. "When I started doing that, it changed my whole life. As I teach in my seminars, your Network can develop only as fast as you do."

Gage's work has continued to evolve, moving now into training Networkers and Networking companies to take advantage of the communication revolution.

"The future will be high-tech," he says. "But it will be high-tech *with* high-touch. It won't be robots calling up and getting orders. It will be the same person telling his or her story, but to thousands of people by satellite instead of to a few people in one room."

Gage's message to Networkers is a familiar one.

"Never give up," he says. "People give up in six months if they're not rich. They go back to what they wanted to escape in the first place. What if it took six years like it took me? Who cares? What is six, versus 40 years?"

JAN RUHE:

Her children were young when Jan Ruhe, then a Dallas homemaker, attended a Discovery Toys party in 1979.

"I fell in love with the product line the first time I saw the toys at a toy party," she says. "I said to myself, 'I will be buying children presents for Christmas and birthdays for the next 15 years. I should get into the toy business. I'll be meeting new mothers, and it will be fun for the children to play with the toys'"

Jan started her business with a $300 gift from her grandmother, two babies under the age of three and another one on the way. She turned a spare bedroom into a demonstration playroom and installed a telephone line.

"Most of the time the meetings were held in my home," she said. "We put up Port-a-cribs and playpens in the bedrooms. We did whatever we had to do to get the job done."

Her early days were often hectic and frustrating, yet in 1980, her first full year in the business, Jan was named Discovery Toys' top manager. She has been at the top of her company ever since. Unfortunately, other types of challenges loomed. In 1985, at the end of an unhappy marriage, Jan entered into a painful and expensive two-year battle for custody of her children. Through it all, she was determined to grow as a business owner and as a person.

"I was listening to tapes by all kinds of speakers, went to many seminars, read thousands of pages on motivation and personal growth," she said, recalling that difficult time. "I read biographies and autobiographies about champions . . . I now realize that only when someone is hungry for information will they go hunting for it."

Jan first sought out those with the survival skills she needed and then began to share her own expertise with others. In 1988, she produced a motivational audio tape set, *"Don't Be Average; Be a Champion,"* and began her Champion Network seminars.

"I could not afford *not* to be self-motivated," she says." I had a responsibility to myself, my team and my family. I started to *think* success. I listened, researched, probed and evaluated. I realized that I was the one to make the final decisions about my business and my life. I did not hesitate to be a pioneer. I began to take risks and make mistakes. I let success, not failure, rub off on me."

Today, Jan Ruhe travels the world with her children and new husband. And she earns well over $200,000 a year. She has sponsored more than 500 people into their own Discovery Toys careers and her downline includes over 6,000 "dynamic, wonderful, excited people."

"The rewards I have achieved in Network Marketing are many," she says. "Network Marketing lets me have the flexibility to work the hours I choose and take off when I need to.

"Network Marketing has changed women's rights. Everyone who participates has the same opportunity, whether or not you have college education . . . whether or not you have support from others.

"There are thousands of people who have become successful in Network Marketing who are willing to show others the light on the trail . . . Break all those past limits. Someone is always winning. It might as well be you."

Today, Jan Ruhe is more than a Network Marketing leader . . . Jan Ruhe is a Champion.

DEAN AND PRISCILLA SMITH:
Priscilla Smith knew what she thought of her husband Dean's idea to start a Network Marketing business. She was dead set

against it. No discussion needed. Her mind was welded shut.

They had tried Network Marketing before, and it hadn't worked for them. Although they did not lose money in the venture, some of their good friends who they had involved in the business had, and Priscilla was determined that would never happen to them.

"I didn't want to be involved at all," she recalls. "I figured that in Network Marketing, very few people at the top make money and then they go out of business.

"Back then, I had a different picture of how to reach success. I had always wanted to be a doctor, but I had to drop out of college because my family didn't have the money. So my one goal was that my own children would be able to go to any college they wanted. And I thought that if Dean brought home a regular paycheck and I brought in a regular paycheck, our children would be able to go to college."

Yet Dean Smith had always wanted to own his own business, and in 1972 had found a company he believed in, Shaklee. After the first argument in their 18 years together, Dean and Priscilla reached an uneasy compromise: Dean would work the business away from home, and Priscilla would ignore it.

"I thought if I would just go along for a few months, the company would go out of business and the problem would go away," she says.

It didn't.

Dean worked hard, and often late into the night, to build his business. One day a few months later, "He came home with a big silly grin on his face and said he had won this trip, and that I couldn't go," Priscilla recalls with a warm laugh.

She did go and somewhere on the chartered flight to Hawaii with 300 other distributors, Priscilla changed her mind.

"It was as if at that moment the weld in my brain broke," she says. "A speck of light came through. I looked around at the other people, and they weren't slick sales types. They weren't talking about money. They were talking about helping people, about how the products had helped people."

The Smiths long ago reached the highest level in their company, and their children did attend the colleges of their choice.

"We've seen our dreams come true, and our expectations greatly exceeded," Priscilla says. Today the Smiths travel the world and Dean Smith, 71, a world champion masters runner, enjoys the time to train and compete.

"I really don't want to retire," he says. "We're living the lifestyle we want, and we can work when we want. I just love to help people achieve, to help people do more than they realize they can do."

"He's more excited about this business now than on day one," Priscilla says. "That's something you don't see too often in the corporate world. Twenty-two years ago, my idea of success was a Fortune 500 company. My attitude was, 'Don't confuse me with the facts.' But it's a whole new world out there. Now, when someone says 'No,' I know it's because they don't 'K-N-O-W.'"

The Smiths urge those considering Network Marketing to do their homework. "So many people don't make the right choice because they don't get enough information to make a good decision," Dean says. "Network Marketing may not be for everybody. I don't believe it is. But it's a tremendous vehicle for people who like to have flexibility and who need to make a good living."

TOM SCHREITER:

Deep in the heart of Texas legend lives one of Network Marketing's greatest teachers: Big Al.

Big Al always knows just what to do. Fumble a presentation or botch an opportunity and Big Al will come through to set things right. Big Al may seem to be larger than life, but he really is alive—in Tom Schreiter's imagination.

Tom's series of "Big Al" books have taught quality Network Marketing to thousands of today's Networkers. Now, Big Al may always know the answers, but the truth is, he learned them all from Tom Schreiter.

Tom has been using his dry sense of humor to teach success principles since the first Big Al book was published in 1985. "I've been basically an introvert, to be quite honest with you," he says. "I'm a pretty quiet, low-key type of guy."

Tom has authored five Big Al books so far. More will follow.

"We wrote the first one because we made all these mistakes," he says in the voice of Big Al's straight man. "Then we made some more mistakes and wrote the second one. We made some more mistakes and wrote the third one; made a *lot* of mistakes and wrote the fourth and fifth ones. Now we're about three books ahead on mistakes. All we basically do is list our mistakes so people can say, 'Yeah, I did that too,' or maybe, 'I can avoid that one.'"

Originally, Tom wrote his books primarily for his downline. So far, they've sold more than 200,000 copies in countries throughout the world. The books have introduced many people to Network Marketing, but they are also one way Tom builds leaders in his own Network business.

"I have a firm belief that multi-level marketing is just building leaders and making them successful," he says. "It means a long-term investment in people. It's not a get-rich-quick thing, yet there's an opportunity to do quite well."

Tom was born on a Nebraska farm. He joined his first Network Marketing company early, in 1972 at age 23. "I got married," he says. "And like most married couples, we needed extra income. I could either work a part-time job until I was 65 to make ends meet or I could have a part-time business in MLM. It was the only business I could afford. Back then, it cost $18.75 to get started—and we financed that."

The Schreiters saw an ad in the paper, went to an opportunity meeting and liked what they saw.

"For the first year and 10 months, we probably were the hardest working couple you ever saw," he says. "We went to every opportunity meeting, every training meeting, every seminar, every company function. We went to a lot of retail presentations and at the end of one year and 10 months, we basically had no customers and no distributors. So, the first year and 10 months were a little bit slow. It took a while before we got our first break."

Yet they never thought of quitting.

"We didn't know we could quit," Tom says. "We didn't have any downline to quit, so we didn't know it was possible. Our sponsor never told us we could quit. We just assumed that was it. Hooked forever. But being naive paid off. After a year and 10 months, we got our first break."

Almost two years after they had started their business, the Schreiters sponsored their first business builder. "That got us some customers and a little momentum to get started," Tom says.

The slow start didn't discourage them, Tom says. The Schreiters had made the decision that first night that Network Marketing was to be their future.

"It's just that we had no skills or any idea how to do it," he says. "Back then, there was no one to provide training. No books, no general training courses." Instead, they learned the old-fashioned way, with plenty of trials and more than a few errors.

"Once, I recruited a guy during jury duty," Tom says. "He came to an opportunity meeting and brought a woman, about age 46, who had 12 children. Her husband was disabled. They lived on $432 a month of government aid.

"The bottom line is, that man dropped out a few months later, but the woman went on to become a superstar, making $20,000, $30,000, $40,000 a year, getting trips and cars. And I ended up making about $1,500 a month on bonuses because I hung in there. Her sponsor dropped out for a $700 a month job."

Tom bases his training on practical, easy-to-duplicate principles that provide a clear picture of what Network Marketing has to offer. He presents it all with a grin and with a realistic idea of what it will take to make it to the top.

And he doesn't promise quick or easy riches.

"What I think works most effectively is to talk about a person who is making $3,000 a month and who makes $1,000 a month part-time on top of that," he says. "In that $3,000 budget, a person may have $100 left over for themselves. By adding $1,000 a month, you've taken that 10 times further."

The additional income can make the difference between financial discomfort and prosperity. "You could throw that $1,000 into the bank and be a millionaire in 20 years," Tom says. "Or you could take a vacation for two to Cancun once a month. There are so many things you can do with $1,000 extra a month. A regular job takes care of all other needs, and this is free money."

Tom looks for potential leaders, for those who are willing to invest effort into their business and into themselves. "The secret to MLM is to build leaders and make them successful," he says. "I look for people who want to become leaders. They may not have the skills yet, but that's okay."

That's when Big Al begins his education process. Tom's advice:

"Scratch out the first six months or a year" to learn the business, be your own best customer, use all your company's products and then, as you learn your business, teach others.

"You're going to invest a lot of time with those you sponsor," he says. "You're going to be a mentor. It's as if I move in with my prospective leaders for five or six months. We'll be doing two-on-one presentations together as they get on-the-job training. And they see they're going to be doing the same thing with *their* leaders to get *them* trained."

At the end of six months, those who make a solid commitment to Network Marketing should be able to make a good presentation and should be working with several potential leaders of their own, Tom says. At the end of their first year, they could have "a couple of very good leaders and $1,000 a month in extra income," as well as a good start on a secure future.

As he talks with people, Tom looks for those who already are attracted to Network Marketing.

"I like to find somebody who *wants* to work the business rather than try to force them to," he says. "While other people spend a lot of time convincing people, I look for someone who doesn't need convincing. They understand it is a business they're going to build, versus a lottery in which they're going to talk to three people and get rich."

Network Marketing has allowed Tom to reach his goals—and to create Big Al. "It's a great industry," he says. "To be quite honest with you, I've gotten a lot more out of it than I've put in."

9
A Beginning

"It is one of the most beautiful compensations of
this life that no man can sincerely try to help
another without helping himself."
— Ralph Waldo Emerson

*The children ran ahead as Tom and Susan Edison stepped off
their jetway and began to climb the brick path toward their house. It
was good to be home.*

*One of the best parts of their business was the chance it gave
them to travel the world, visiting associates who long ago had become friends. But another was the opportunity to return, as always, here to their home. After a couple of weeks away, a huge glass
house in the middle of a high Colorado meadow seemed just the
place to be.*

*"Andy and Samantha looked good, didn't they?" Susan asked Tom,
unconsciously reaching out for his hand as they walked. "I think she's
right. Her new group is going to take off. Looks like the next few
months will be busy ones for her—and for me."*

*"You've taught her well," Tom said. "And her top level people are
fireballs. You'll probably be able to handle most of your end from here,
don't you think?"*

"Yes. I don't plan to stir for the entire winter. There are too many things I want to do here. Like gaze into a fire."

Tom laughed. "I've heard that before," he said. "Remember what you used to say when you were first starting the business? 'I can inch my way to the top where I am or I can fly to the top on my own.' You've really taken flight, Sue."

Susan squeezed his hand and laughed. "You thought I was crazy," she said. "It took you two years to admit I hadn't taken leave of every single one of my senses. Remember my first bonus check? Not quite $4."

She paused. "Where do you suppose we would have ended up if we hadn't become Networkers?" she asked.

"Wherever it would have been, it would have been okay," Tom said, as they reached their deck. "We would have made sure of that. I'm just glad we made the choices we did when we did. Come on, do you want to order a movie or screen the new product holograms. David said he'd have them here this evening."

"You go ahead," Susan said, sinking into a chair beside the pool. "I'm going to sit here for a few minutes and watch the sun set."

Dusk gathered as Susan leaned back in her chair and thought back to their trip and to the friends they had visited. Tomorrow would be a busy day . . .

As the meadow darkened, the lights inside the house began to cast brighter reflections into the hydropool until they seemed to pull her inside to her family.

"Look back?" she said to herself as she got up and turned to the house. "No. Not ever."

THE DISTANCE BETWEEN OURSELVES and our futuristic friend, Susan Edison, may not be that great. Networking companies are already using satellite technology to revolutionize the way they communicate with distributors and with those who want to learn more about their company and products.

One example is The Peoples Network. As the only television network in the world devoted exclusively to personal development, TPN beams solution-oriented television directly into homes via satellite, providing a positive alternative to what many are calling "an out-of-control media."

Recognized experts, teachers, coaches, motivators, and leaders appear daily in programming that covers: Finance, Health and Wellness, Family and Parenting, Business and Career Issues, Professional Development, Individual Growth, and much more.

The company, co-founded by Jeff Olson and Eric Worre, appears to be on to something and has already attracted the attention of publishing giant Simon and Schuster, *Entrepreneur* magazine and *The Wall Street Journal.*

In addition to personal developmental programming, TPN is taking its concept one step further, by creating the world's first "virtual mall"—what Mr. Olson refers to as "collaborative economics"—providing other manufacturers' products, goods and services directly to the end consumer using satellite technology to inform, and UPS to deliver.

USANA Corp. which distributes health and wellness products, already uses the World Wide Web to educate and inform its distributors as well as potential customers 24-hours a day. And with over 400,000 "hits" per month, the USANA home page is proving to be another example of the way our world will work in the future.

And lest we forget, industry leader Amway has been using CD-ROM technology for a number of its product catalogs for a few years now . . .

We believe these high-technology approaches to business herald the communication and business revolution that lies ahead.

Technology already is cutting new frontiers through the way we live our lives, until it seems that our futures are racing toward us at the speed of light. Even though we sometimes feel we are whirling in a confusion of change, we know the decisions we make today will shape all else that is to come.

Like those early in the century who watched with awe the approach of Halley's Comet, we all can choose to view the future with apprehension or, with knowledge and an open mind—with awe and anticipation.

That is your choice.

When a brand new century finds Susan Edison on her Colorado mountaintop, we believe those who today choose Network Marketing also will find themselves looking out over their own vistas of opportunity and accomplishment.

That is your *Future Choice.*

Postscript

AS YOU MAKE THE CHOICES that shape your future, our thoughts and good wishes go with you. We invite you to learn more about Network Marketing and about how your own networking business can help you build the life you desire. We've listed a number of excellent resources in the back of this book and how you can obtain them.

And please, contact us directly as well. If we don't know the answers to your questions, we'll help you find them. That's how Network Marketing works. Neighbor to neighbor, new friend to new friend.

Michael S. Clouse
Kathie Jackson Anderson
Future Choice
PO Box 55455
Seattle, Washington 98155
E-mail: msc@swswsw.com

Appendix A:
To Learn More About . . .

Network Marketing

All the books listed below may be obtained through the *Upline® Resources* catalog. To receive a complete *Upline® Resources* catalog, send your name and address to:
Upline / MLM Publishing, 215 4th St NE, Charlottesville, VA 22902.

Clouse, Michael S., *Business is Booming*, 1996.

Clouse, Michael S., Editor in Chief, *Upline®* magazine (monthly)

Fogg, John Milton. *The Greatest Networker in the World*, 1993.

Hutton, Shirley, *Pay Yourself What You're Worth*, Bantam Books, 1988.

Kalench, John, *17 Secrets of the Master Prospectors*, 1994.

Kalench, John, *The Greatest Opportunity in the History of the World*, 1991.

Kalench, John, *Being the Best You Can Be in MLM* 1992.

Schreiter, Tom, *Big Al's How to Build MLM Leaders for Fun and Profit*, 1991.

Schreiter, Tom, *Big Al's How to Create a Recruiting Explosion*, 186.

Schreiter, Tom, *Big Al Tells All*, 1985.

Poe, Richard, *Wave 3*, 1994.

Audio and Video Training Sets

Clear Image, Inc., *It's About Time*, 1996. (video)

Gage, Randy, *How to Earn $100,000 a Year in Network Marketing*, 1992, rev. 1996. (audio)

Maloney, Dayle, *Secrets of Multi-Level Marketing, Vol. I & II*, 1989. (audio)

Millionaires in Motion, *Network Marketing: Your Magic Carpet to Personal and Financial Freedom*, 1992. (video)

Nightingale, Earl, *The Strangest Secret*, 1987 (audio)

Success in Action, *Network Marketing in Action*, 1991. (audio)

Books on Business Trends

Aburdene, Patricia and Naisbitt, John, *Megatrends for Women*, 1992.

Branson, Robert M. Ph.D., *Coping with the Fast Track Blues: A Survival Guide for your Climb to the Top*, 1989.

Celente, Gerald, *Trend Tracking*, 1990.

Clason, George, *The Richest Man in Babylon*, 1955

Clifton, Donald O. and Nelson, Paula, *Soar With Your Strengths*, 1992

Edwards, Paul and Sarah, *Getting Business to Come to You*, 1981.

Edwards, Paul and Sarah, *Making It On Your Own*, 1991.

Eisenson, Marc, *The Banker's Secret*, 1990.

Gross, Andrea, *Shifting Gears· Planning a New Strategy for Midlife*, 1991

Hollowell, Edward M, M.D. and Grace, William J. Jr., *What Are You Worth?*, 1989.

Holland, Philip, *How To Start a Business Without Quitting Your Job*, 1992.

Popcorn, Faith, *The Popcorn Report*, 1991.

Popcorn, Faith, *Clicking*, 1996

Whitlock, Charles R., *How to Get Rich*, 1991.

Special thanks to: John Milton Fogg, Scott DeGarmo, Randy Gage, Jan Ruhe, Tom Schreiter, Dean and Priscilla Smith, Lynn and Darryl Kuntz, Jason Boreyko, Kelly Thayer, September Clouse, Taylor Clouse, Ashley Clouse, Cary Falk, Miles and Kathleen Jackson, Alexandra, Brooke, Jill and Rob Nixon and Bev Habib.

Appendix B: Overcome the No-Time Syndrome

Millions of networkers are building a successful part-time business in their spare time. How often have you heard, "I'd like to, but I just don't have the time"? There are 168 hours in every single week. Where does the time go? Take a look:

Activity	Time Spent		Time remaining in the week
Sleep:	8 hours/day	56 hours/week	112 hours
Full time job:	8 hours/day	40 hours/week	72 hours
Commuting:	2 hours/day	10 hours/week	62 hours
Eating:	2 hours/day	14 hours/week	48 hours
Family and entertainment:	2 hours/day	14 hours/week	34 hours
Miscellaneous:	2 hours/day	14 hours/week	20 hours

According to a recent A.C. Nielsen survey, the average American watches 49 hours of television per week. How much is the TV habit costing you? $5,000 a year? $10,000 a year? More? Kicking the TV habit could make you rich.

"I gave up television," said Eunice Vinberg, a top Network Marketer. "I decided I could watch 'Lifestyles of the Rich and Famous' now, or live it later."

Appendix C: Ethics

1. Today's quality Network Marketing companies *offer legitimate goods and services at fair prices.* The company's primary goal is to get its products to the end user, the wholesale or retail consumer.

2. *Compensation is based on sales, not recruitment.* Distributors earn commissions and bonuses based on the amount of sales, either individual or in their group. Payments are not made for recruiting alone.

3. *Sale of goods and services must be the company's primary focus, not the growth of its distribution network.*

4. Legitimate network companies do *not require distributors to buy large amounts of inventory with which to begin a business.* And they offer liberal buy-back policies in the event a distributor chooses to leave the business.

5. *Unreasonable claims about the amount of income possible from Network Marketing are prohibited.* Although the rewards to a successful marketer can be staggering, those in the company and its networks are diligent in fairly presenting income opportunities. Network Marketing is not a get-rich-quick scheme.

As any business venture, it rewards those who are willing to work hard and who display persistence and creativity.

6. Look for a *proven management track record*. Whether it is a company that has been around for years or one that has just begun, look for a record of successful top management. Some of today's most exciting start-up companies are the product of years of experience by industry leaders who are introducing improvements and innovation into Network Marketing.

The DSA, MLMIA, the Federal Trade Commission, state attorneys general and other consumer groups offer additional information on how to judge Network Marketing and other business opportunities.

Index